OUTL...
New ...

"If saving money is your concern, this updated guide is a big help."

— *Yankee* magazine

"Recommended first aid for your personal economy."
— *Antique & The Arts Weekly*

"This is a handy book to keep in the car on any trip to New England—even if you don't think you'll be doing any shopping. . . . The book will save you much more than it costs."
— *Hudson Valley Magazine*

"An accurate and detailed listing of each and every good, reliable, and useful outlet store in New England."
— *The Newtown* (Conn.) *Bee*

"Where to save one's money and have a fun shopping spree to boot. Picking up a copy . . . could save someone a lot of money."

— *Maine Book Review*

OUTLET GUIDE:
New England

Connecticut, Maine, Massachusetts, New Hampshire, Rhode Island, and Vermont

Ninth Edition

by A. Miser and A. Pennypincher

A Voyager Book

The Globe Pequot Press

Old Saybrook, Connecticut

Library of Congress Cataloging-in-Publication Data

Miser, A.
    Outlet guide: New England : Connecticut, Maine, Massachusetts, New
Hampshire, Rhode Island, and Vermont / by A. Miser and A. Pennypincher.
— 9th ed.
        p. cm.
    Previous ed. published under title: Factory outlet guide to New England.
    Includes index.
    ISBN 1-56440-639-3
    1. Outlet stores—New England—Directories. I. Pennypincher, A.
II. Title.
HF5429.4.A11M57 1995
381'.45'02574—dc20   94-43254
                                                                           CIP

Manufactured in the United States of America
Ninth Edition/Third Printing

Contents

Contents

Introduction

As you look for ways to stretch your budget, the outlet option is one we strongly recommend to you. When you shop at outlets, you can shop at "sale" prices throughout the entire year. It is realistic to say that, in the course of a year, you could either save 50 percent of your budget for clothing, gifts, and household items or—the other side of the coin— you could spend your budget but buy twice as much.

Do not assume that outlets have only low-quality or undesirable merchandise. Many prestigious manufacturers use this marketing approach. As you browse through this book, you will see innumerable well-known brand names. Manufacturers from all levels have tried the water and decided the swimming is definitely inviting!

When we first began researching factory stores in the early 1960s, they were few and far between. They were inside the factories themselves and were often little more than an unused space converted into a makeshift sales area. Even the manufacturers weren't too sure about this aspect of their business life. Eventually, as more and more people discovered the bargains in factory stores, the sales areas were tidied up, manufacturers started to advertise their locations, and factory store shopping slowly became respectable.

Alert manufacturers soon sensed the latent potential in this marketing approach and learned to capitalize on it. The conversion of once-busy, but now idle, floor space led to the mill developments we see in Fall River, Lawrence, and New Bedford, Massachusetts, as well as Norwalk and Bridgeport, Connecticut, and the mall and cluster developments with their focus on direct factory stores and distributors, such as those in Kittery, Maine and North Conway, New Hampshire.

Today the task of seeking relief from inflation has been greatly simplified for the shopper. There are numerous clusters of outlets that offer extraordinary shopping opportunities for everyone. You can go to these complexes and find easy parking and a diversity of top-quality outlets carrying everything from toys to shoes at savings of 25 to 70 percent. You will shop in attractive surroundings and go home with twice as much for your money as a trip to your normal department store would yield.

There still remain stores in factories themselves, but they are invariably clean, attractive, and usually well stocked. They may not have luxurious fixtures, but then you are not buying the fixtures. As a matter of fact, with malls in such abundance, real factory stores can be a lot of fun.

Planning Your Shopping Trip

Here are our suggestions for a productive outlet shopping expedition.

Take a small loose-leaf notebook and divide it into sections. One section should be for each person for whom you buy clothing or anything else during the course of the year; jot down sizes, needs, and desires. Another section should be for your home on a room-by-room basis. Keep additional pages for other categories as the need arises. With such pertinent information on hand, you can go shopping with confidence.

When you are clothes shopping for adults at an outlet, you can afford to think in terms of "investment" clothing. Suits for men and women, as well as overcoats and sport jackets, fall into this category. An expensive suit should be expected to last for years; for it to do so requires that you have carefully studied the styling, quality, and tailoring details. You can also afford to supplement your basic wardrobe with less expensive items that reflect the whims of fashion. A blouse in the current "in" shades can be discarded when fashion dictates a new shade; you won't feel so wasteful if that blouse cost only a few dollars at an outlet. But remember, an item that will never be worn is not a good buy, no matter how low the price!

Use your notebook for essential information about your home, such as window sizes, color schemes, fabric and wallpaper samples (tape swatches in your notebook), and furniture needs. You will find many outlets selling a variety of items for the home; if you see a marvelous buy on one of your trips, but you aren't sure about measurements or colors, your "find" will be of little use. Also, be sure to take along a tape measure.

Be sure your notebook includes a list of the people for whom you buy gifts. Do you have a birthday celebration, a wedding, a graduation, a new baby in the offing? Put all these events in your book; you will find endless possibilities for low-cost gifts in outlets. Your prospective holiday gift list definitely should be included so you can shop for Christmas presents all year round.

Once you have all your planning and listing completed, allow yourself some time to browse in local department stores to get a feel for prices, current styles, colors, and so on. Catalogs will also help you in this respect. Now you are ready to go outlet shopping. One final thought: Consider including a shopping trip in a vacation. You may find that your savings on a major buying trip, such as before the opening of school, will help you pay for your vacation.

Using This Book

We have included only a few types of stores in this book. A direct factory outlet, such as the Mikasa outlet, is owned by the manufacturer and offers its merchandise at wholesale or close-to-wholesale prices. A manufacturer's or distributor's outlet is one in which a group of manufacturers offer their products to the public at less than the suggested retail price. Famous Footwear is an example of such an outlet. Off-price stores, in which enterprising retailers offer closeouts, overruns, or seconds from numerous manufacturers, offer many of the advantages that outlets do. As a service to our readers, we are including a new appendix of a select group of these "deep discounters" located in New England. (See page 208.)

We have used a star (*) in the left-hand margin to alert you to a special city or town for outlet shopping.

Independent Yankees that they are, many outlet malls will not have central telephone numbers. If the phone number is not listed in the guide due to space restrictions, call one of the following area codes and the general number for information (555–1212) and request the appropriate town and outlet store:

Connecticut (203)
Maine (207)
Massachusetts (617) or (508) or (413)
New Hampshire (603)
Rhode Island (401)
Vermont (802)

Take a good atlas with you when you are traveling to a new area. We have provided brief directions to many of the outlets, but you will still find a road atlas a necessity (unless you actually like to stop at gas stations and ask questions).

Almost all outlets take MasterCard and Visa. Some take American Express. More and more are taking Discover as we go to press. Most outlets will take personal checks with proper identification. And cash is still accepted. Check with individual stores if a listing for credit cards or personal checks does not appear in this book.

Outlet retailers are making a real attempt to make their stores handicapped accessible. Most new outlets are on one level and have handicapped ramps and wide doors. Please call ahead if there is any question as to handicapped accessibility, particularly if you are interested in a special outlet.

You won't starve while you are in outlet-land. Most complexes have one or more restaurants on site. Most outlets are within a mile or two of a fast-food restaurant or coffee shop. If you know you will be shopping during mealtime and have special preferences, check out the area, either by calling or by scouting in a car.

State Tourism Information

If your group is interested in sponsoring a bus tour, call the chamber of commerce of the area you wish to visit. Call the state tourism office (see below) when an outlet mall telephone number is not listed in this book.

For information on accommodations, attractions, historical sites, and recreation in New England, contact:

Connecticut Department of Economic Development
Tourism Division
865 Brook Street
Rocky Hill, CT 06067–3405
(800) CT–BOUND (800–282–6863)

Maine Department of Economic and Community Development
Office of Tourism
Statehouse Station #59
Augusta, ME 04333
(207) 287–2656

Massachusetts Office of Travel and Tourism
100 Cambridge Street, Thirteenth Floor
Boston, MA 02202
(617) 727–3201

New Hampshire Office of Travel and Tourism
105 Loudon Road, P.O. Box 856
Concord, NH 03301
(603) 271–2666

Rhode Island Department of Economic Development
Tourism Division
7 Jackson Walkway
Providence, RI 02903
(401) 277–2601
(800) 556–2484

Vermont Agency of Development and Community Affairs
Travel Division
134 State Street
Montpelier, VT 05602
(802) 828–3237

NOTE: No outlet owner may purchase inclusion in this book. Store inclusion is purely a personal decision on the part of the authors. In addition, some outlets chose not to participate in the compilation of this book, and providing pertinent information was on a purely voluntary basis. Consequently, the extent of information may vary from profile to profile and outlet to outlet. If you have discovered an outlet not included in this book, please contact the authors for inclusion in the next edition. We are always snooping around for great outlet finds for our readers. Kindly write to:

A. Miser and A. Pennypincher
c/o The Globe Pequot Press
P.O. Box 833
Old Saybrook, CT 06475

Wishing you happy outlet shopping!

A. Miser   A. Pennypincher

In compiling this book we have made every attempt to provide accurate information. Outlets do, however, go out of business, sometimes close for vacation, change hours, and even move. Do not go any great distance unless you check first to see if things have changed. There is nothing more disappointing than being where an outlet isn't or being where an outlet is when it's closed.

Many towns in New England are affected by tourism, and store hours will fluctuate to benefit from the influx of seasonal visitors. Be prepared for such extensions or for a reduction of hours in the off-season. Again, call ahead if a particular outlet is of importance to you.

Profiles

Accessory Factory
Do you need that special accessory to complete an outfit? Here women's handbags, belts, scarves, jewelry, and hair accessories are offered at 20 to 40 percent off retail prices.

Adams Mill
You will spot a variety of favorite brand names here, including Carter's and OskKosh B'Gosh, as well as Health-Tex and Bugle Boy. For girls there are skirts, blouses, sportswear, and outerwear; for boys you'll find sweaters, pants, and outerwear, all at savings from 25 to 50 percent.

Adolfo II
Ladies knitwear by Aldofo II, Rafael, Donna Toran, and Dressy Tessy. Savings up to 70 percent.

Adrienne Vittadini
Here you will find fashions for women from Adrienne Vittadini, along with fashionable accessories, often at 40 percent off retail prices.

Aileen
Aileen offers casual women's sportswear, most of it knitwear and all made in the United States. Petite, misses', and women's sizes sell at 35 to 70 percent off retail.

Alessi & Bourgeat
Alessi stainless-steel espresso coffeemakers, holloware, barware, and flatware are available for the connoisseur at big savings off retail prices, as are Bourgeat pots and pans of stainless steel, copper, and aluminum.

Alpine Sheets and Towels
Featured here are Fieldcrest, Royal Velvet towels, and Bates bedspreads among the selection. Savings of 20 to 60 percent off retail. UPS shipping.

American Broadloom Braided Rug and Furniture Company
If you like the colonial look in home decorating, you will like the braided rugs and furniture available here at substantial savings.

American Home Sewing
Sewing needs, and a museum right in the store.

American Tourister
Traditional and soft-sided luggage, garment bags, sports bags, and business cases at 40 to 70 percent off suggested retail prices. Also available are travel accessories by Remington, luggage carts, and Buxton wallets. If you are going on a trip, sending someone off to college, or starting a new business venture, you can fill many of your needs here.

Amherst Sports
Women's sportswear, including skirts, shirts, slacks, and Dean's classic sweaters. Savings of 20 to 30 percent off retail.

Anne Klein
How exciting to find designer clothing at bargain-basement prices! Here you will find an excellent array of the clothes that have made Anne Klein such a popular name. You'll even find the accessories you'll need to make your look complete. Savings are 20 to 50 percent off retail.

Ann Taylor
Fine apparel and shoes for women, featuring Tahari and Nichole Miller in addition to the Ann Taylor label.

Arrow
Men's dress and sport shirts, slacks, shorts, sweaters, ties, and accessories. Save 20 to 50 percent off Arrow and Gold Toe brands.

Arrow Paper Party Store
The next time you have a party or holiday event approaching, be sure to take a trip to the Party Store. It offers an extensive selection of the paper goods distributed by Arrow Paper Company. Paper plates, tablecloths, napkins, cups, crepe paper, streamers, and a variety of other holiday party-oriented items are available here, at savings of 10 to 25 percent.

The Artisan Outlet

The Artisan Outlet might be compared to a department store of clothing or an upscale specialty store. You can choose from such top-level brand names as Evan-Picone, Liz Claiborne, Anne Klein, Chaps by Ralph Lauren, Burberry, and Christian Dior all at savings of up to 50 percent.

Bag and Baggage

Moderate to better handbags, wallets, briefcases, luggage, accessories, and executive gifts. Savings are 20 to 50 percent.

Bagmakers

Handbags, casual luggage, briefcases, backpacks, and wallets at savings up to 60 percent. Brand names you will find here are Borelli, Etienne Aigner, John Romain, Palana, and Stone Mountain.

Bag Outlet

Stuffco International offers its full line of handbags and soft luggage at its store, the Bag Outlet. You will find a variety of nationally known brand names in the extensive selection of high-quality items. Savings range from 30 to 50 percent.

Banana Republic

Safari-style sportswear, heavy on the khaki, for men and women. Hats, accessories, and travel gear for the safari and outdoors. All at substantial savings. This is a very upscale outlet.

Banister Shoe

This store carries brands such as Capezio, Red Cross, Selby, and Cobbie, both seconds and first quality, at savings of up to 50 percent. You'll certainly be satisfied with these casual, dress, and athletic shoes for men and women.

Barbizon Lingerie

Since 1917 Barbizon has been manufacturing excellent lingerie. Now you can save money and be a part of this longstanding tradition by shopping at this outlet. You'll save up to 70 percent on first-quality daywear and sleepwear featuring Cuddleskin, Featheraire, and Blendaire Batiste fabrics.

Barnes Window Treatment

You will find hundreds of yards of fabric for home decorating at savings of 60 to 75 percent at Barnes. Remnants, closeouts, and on-the-bolt fabrics from a variety of manufacturers are available here.

Barneys New York

Very "today" apparel, shoes, and accessories for men and women. Choose from designs of Giorgio Armani or DKNY, among others, or Barneys private label, all at savings of 30 to 70 percent.

The Barn of Lieff

The excellent fabric selection at the Barn includes drapery and slipcover yard goods. Fabrics by leading manufacturers are available at savings of 40 percent and more. The selection, the generous savings, and the attentive sales personnel are factors that make this store well worth a visit.

Barns of Bradford

If you are looking for new furniture in colonial or traditional styling, a trip to the Barns of Bradford, where solid pine, oak, and cherry furniture are offered, may be helpful. In addition to the Bradford brand, you will find Nathan Hale, Crawford, Norwalk, and more. Savings range between 25 and 60 percent.

Bartlett Yarns

For anyone interested in yarns for various handcrafts, a visit here is an experience. All-wool yarns are available for knitters, spinners, weavers, and craftspeople who prefer the sturdiness, strength, and springy resiliency of wool. A variety of colors and types is available. The 10 to 50 percent savings are helpful to any handcrafter. Some blankets are also in stock.

The mill, dating back to 1821, is open to visitors and is very interesting to see.

Bass

This well-known shoe factory has been making shoes for more than one hundred years and has earned a reputation for its quality and workmanship. At the outlet stores you will find Bass shoes, boots, and loafers in a wonderful range of styles and sizes. Both rejects and closeouts are available at savings of 20 to 50 percent. You also will find socks, belts, handbags, chamois shirts, and related items. Some outlets carry a full line of outdoor "Lifestyle" wear for men and women.

Bates Mill Store
The Bates Mill is the largest plant in the world for jacquard-woven bedspreads. It is also the most integrated facility of its kind, as it carries out all the stages in bedspread production.

The store offers a wide selection of Bates bedspreads, as well as mattress pads, blankets, towels, and sheets carrying such labels as Fieldcrest, St. Mary's, Pepperell, and others. The items are closeout styles and irregulars. A broad choice of styles, colors, and sizes is available at savings of 30 to 40 percent.

Bed & Bath
First-quality and irregular towels, sheets, comforters, and bedspreads from Laura Ashley, Martex, Utica, and Wamsutta, among others. Discounts range from 40 to 70 percent.

Bed, Bath, and Beyond
Fine linens and accessories for the bedroom, bathroom, and home from famous manufacturers at 20 to 40 percent off.

Benetton
Get some color in your wardrobe with a stop at this popular outlet. Your teenagers will definitely demand to stop here. You'll be glad you did when you see the savings on this colorful Italian sportswear for men, women, and children.

Bennington Potters
Bennington Potters has an excellent reputation for its fine stoneware. Its distinctive Bennington mark is found on the underside of all its pieces, helping to identify future heirlooms. This is an outstanding place to shop for yourself or for gifts because mugs, dinnerware, pitchers, and home accessories are here in profusion. Overruns, discontinued items, and seconds are all available, and savings are 20 to 50 percent.

Bidermann
Menswear from Burberry, Yves St. Laurent, Arrow, and Gold Toe with savings from 30 to 70 percent.

Big Dog
Adults' and children's Big Dog tees, sweatshirts, and more with the familiar black-and-white canine logo, all at outlet prices.

Black & Decker
Black & Decker tools have always been known for their top quality. This outlet carries Black & Decker power and hand tools and the Black & Decker line of small home appliances, such as toasters, irons, and toaster ovens. You will find savings up to 80 percent on blemished and reconditioned products. The reconditioned items carry a full warranty. Men love this outlet.

Bogner
Ladies' designer sportswear, ladies' and men's golfwear, and accessories at outlet prices.

Bon Worth
At Bon Worth you will find ladies' sportswear and coordinates in brands you will recognize. Discounted separates come in misses sizes 6–20 and plus sizes 34–46.

The Book and Music Outlet
This outlet will become a favorite habit once you visit and see the money you can save. The kids will definitely be more interested in this store than other bookstores because it offers 10 to 80 percent discounts on cassettes and compact discs.

Book Warehouse
Book Warehouse offers overruns of books from major publishers at 50 to 90 percent off retail prices. You will also find related items such as calendars, atlases, and IBM-compatible software.

Bose
High-quality stereo electronics direct from the manufacturer, including

speakers, CD players, and more. At least 20 percent off factory-renewed equipment.

Boston Traders

This crisp line of fine sportswear for men, women, and children is offered at savings of 30 to 50 percent off suggested retail prices. There are men's big and tall sizes, too.

Brooks Brothers

Brooks Brothers, established in 1818, is one of the oldest clothing stores in the U.S. At the outlet, you can buy exclusive, quality business dress and sportswear made with the finest materials, all at a nice discount. There is a classic selection of suits and more for both men and women.

Bugle Boy

This popular label is sewn into great casual wear: jeans, slacks, shirts, T-shirts, and more. At this outlet you will find savings on styles for boys in sizes 4 to 7, for girls in sizes 4 to 6, and in juniors', misses', young men's, and men's sizes.

B.U.M.

Build Up Muscle (B.U.M.) with men's, women's, and children's activewear at up to 50 percent off retail.

Buttons and Things

No button about it! If you like to sew or have burst some buttons that need to be replaced, then you should stop at this helpful store. The staff will introduce you to an array of sewing accessories, crafts, collector's thimbles, Christmas collectibles, and unique gifts—not to mention buttons of every shape, size, and design. It's mind-boggling. Savings are up to 75 percent off retail prices.

Calvin Klein

This store carries the complete lines of Calvin Klein top-quality sportswear and accessory items at savings of 30 to 50 percent. You can find lots of clothing for all members of the family, for there are innumerable choices. A great place to shop—even if you don't look exactly like a Calvin Klein model.

Cambridge Dry Goods
Classic coordinated activewear, sportswear, and career wear for women at savings of 30 to 70 percent.

Cape Isle Knitters
Top-drawer sweaters and knits for men and women at savings of 30 to 60 percent.

Carter's
Carter's offers clothing for children. Sizes go from newborn to 14 in an extensive selection of clothing for all purposes. A variety of name brands, including Carter's, is featured here, and all are priced to please your budget.

Cascade Woolen Mill
Featured at this store is an outstanding assortment of over 200 styles and colors of all-wool fabrics made at the mill. If you like to sew, the range of patterns and colors should provide ample inspiration for skirts, suits, blazers, and pants, and the savings of 40 to 50 percent will make quite a difference in the total cost.

Casual Corner
Excellent savings from this fine specialty store for women. Coats, suits, dresses, separates, and accessories, all at outlet prices.

Casual Male/Big and Tall
Discounts of 30 to 60 percent on men's brand-name and designer fashions for hard-to-fit sizes. Stop here if you have a big guy in the family.

Catamount Glass
Catamount offers its own unique line of glass cookware in its factory store. Made from borosilica, the glassware is flameproof, microwave-safe, dishwasher-safe, and uniquely attractive. Available in casseroles, cooking pots, double boilers, warmers, soufflé dishes, steamers, measuring cups, mugs, and pitchers, this glassware is extremely useful and practical. The savings of 30 to 50 percent are an added attraction.

CB Sports
Prestige skiwear for the entire family at substantial savings. CB jackets, turtlenecks, headbands—you'll find them all here.

Champion/Hanes
Color is the keynote here—the brighter the better. You will find the current season's most popular colors in sweats, T-shirts, and socks. First-quality merchandise and seconds at good savings.

Chaus
If you admire Chaus apparel in specialty and department stores, here is the place to buy it at substantial savings. Women's clothing by J. Chaus is available in petite, misses', and women's sizes.

Cherry Lane (Cannon)
For super savings on Cannon brand towels, sheets, pillows, blankets, place mats, and related linens, be sure to check this outlet store. Both first-quality and irregular merchandise are offered.

Chicago Cutlery
Fine American cutlery on the cutting edge. Knife sets, complete with wooden storage blocks. Other kitchen accessories, all at outlet prices.

The Children's Outlet
You and your child will have a delightful time shopping in this store. You'll find brand names such as Health-Tex, OshKosh B'Gosh, Ocean Pacific, Lee, Nike, Our Girl, and J. J. Poole, all at a welcome savings of 30 to 40 percent.

China Fair Warehouse
With savings of 50 percent or more, this outlet store offers an unbelievable variety of imported contemporary glass, dinnerware, and cookware. There are over 3,000 items in stock, including such helpful gadgets as French vegetable steamers, Copco teakettles, and cast-iron cookware. A must visit for home chefs and a tradition for Boston college students setting up a home-away-from-home; you're sure to find something you like at this store.

Christian Dior
Fashions for men and women by Christian Dior. Also fragrances, lingerie, handbags, jewelry, and other accessories. Christian Dior fine china, crystal, and gift pieces are also available. All merchandise is 25 to 50 percent off retail prices.

Chuck Roast
Chuck Roast is *the* skiwear designer of North Conway, New Hampshire. At the outlet you will find overruns at substantial savings.

Church's English Shoes
This store features an excellent variety of men's shoes, with many styles, sizes, and colors available. There are boots, dress shoes, and casual styles such as loafers in a range of sizes and widths from A to triple E. They are priced at approximately 20 percent below retail cost.

Coach
The famous Coach leatherwear is now available at outlet prices. You will find handbags, such as the classic Tailored Pouch, Drawstring Sack, Town Bag, or Spectator. These finely crafted handbags, as well as wallets, briefcases, belts, gloves, and other accessories for men and women, are offered at savings of up to 50 percent off retail.

Cohoes, Ltd.
Top designer names in a very attractive store. This outlet offers savings of 20 to 25 percent on top-of-the-line brands for apparel.

Cole-Haan Shoes
Fine footwear, apparel, and accessories at less than department store prices.

Colonial Candle of Cape Cod
Candles in a variety of colors, sizes, and shapes. Also a selection of accessories for the home with savings for you.

Coloratura
Women's avant-garde apparel and accessories. Trendy separates made of all-natural fibers. Savings from 30 to 60 percent.

Colours by Alexander Julian
Current fashions from Colours or Coloursport for men or children. Savings from this American designer are 30 to 60 percent off retail.

The Company Store
Here are good clothes and accessories at prices that won't make you end up "owing your soul to the company store." The Company Store offers a selection of clothing for men and women, as well as ties and belts; you will recognize Woolrich and Pulitzer among the quality brands available here. Savings are 20 to 40 percent.

Connecticut Gift
Originally this store was in two parts, the Rockwell factory store for silver and Connecticut House Pewterers. There are sterling silver or glass items, pewter giftware, pewter miniature animals, glass giftware, and a variety of other gift items. This is a nice place to shop for a wedding present, and the savings are 20 to 50 percent.

Converse
Converse ships its popular sports shoes that aren't quite perfect to its factory outlets, where basketball, tennis, running, and field sports shoes are offered at savings of 30 to 50 percent or more.

Corning/Revere
The famous Revere and Corning products are found at savings of 30 to 40 percent. The copper-bottomed or aluminum-disk bottomed pots and pans or the all-copper items will perk up anyone's kitchen, as will the well-designed Corning items. Some of the items sold here as premium seconds have only a slight defect. To the untrained eye, most appear to be perfect.

Cotton Mill
Curtains, draperies, towels, comforters, blankets, sheets, and bedspreads from Bates, J. P. Stevens, Lady Pepperell, Dundee, Burlington, Martex, and other manufacturers. Savings of 50 percent. Bring your measurements for custom designs.

Crabtree and Evelyn

British specialties, from orange marmalade and teas to Beatrix Potter soaps and fancy sachets. Prices much lower than at boutiques.

Crate and Barrel

This well-known purveyor of home and home-entertaining wares offers overstocks at good savings. You will find many attractive items you may have seen in their catalog. Terra-cotta bowls, European ceramic tableware, and handsome outdoor furniture are among the contemporary offerings available.

Creative Playthings

Durable wooden swing sets from Creative Playthings. Choose from more than a dozen styles of heavy duty climbing and swing combinations. Provide years of fun for the kids at savings from 15 to 50 percent off regular prices.

Crockett Collection

Traditional greeting cards silk-screened in a country motif. Savings from 30 to 50 percent.

Cuddletown

Comforters, pillows, and gift items, as well as European-style equipment for filling comforters, pillows, and more with down. Outlet prices on discontinued items and seconds.

Cuddle Toys by Douglas

This store has been a longtime favorite of ours. It is worth a visit not only for children, but for all the rest of us who are young at heart.

The stuffed toys are of all sizes and descriptions. Some are musical. If you are a doting grandparent, parent, or relative, you'll surely find a toy here to delight that special child. If you are a collector, you will find many wonderful specimens. And the savings of 20 to 50 percent are an added bonus.

Curious Cargo (Orzeck Corporation)

The store carries an attractive line of poured-composition statuary and wall-decor items. Included are lamps as well as figurines, which range from gulls to sailors to lighthouses. Savings here range from 25 to 40 percent.

Curtain Factory Outlet
First-quality and discontinued styles of curtains, drapes, bedspreads, ensembles, window accessories, and shower curtains. Substantial savings.

Curtains Plus
Curtains Plus offers a nice selection of curtains and other window dressings to brighten up any room in the house. You will also find coordinating linens for that decorator look. The savings are generous.

Dan Howard's Maternity Factory Outlet
The selection and the styles are suited to a variety of needs, ranging from casual slacks and tops to stylish dresses and separates. Savings range from 30 to 50 percent—such a help when you're buying clothes for a short-term use.

Dansk
The long-popular Dansk products are arrayed at the Dansk outlet store. The wide selection of cookware and kitchen items, as well as giftware, makes shopping here a delightful experience. Everything from candle holders to dishes are on display at savings of 25 to 50 percent. The helpful sales personnel and the excellent selection make this outlet a "satisfactory" experience.

Danskin
Dancewear, leotards, and tights for women and children at savings.

Dan's Pine Shop
Occasional tables, coffee tables, cribbage tables, storage units, and even a rocking horse are available here in both dark and honey-tone finishes; many pieces have hand-painted flower designs.

You will also find furniture made of other materials from other famous manufacturers: Nathan Hale, Benton Brothers, and Kemple Stuart are among those supplementing the pine furniture. All furniture here is available at a savings of approximately 30 percent.

Profiles

Decker's

Decker's is the factory store for the Gant manufacturing company. Here you will find an excellent stock of clothing, including shirts, sweaters, belts, and ties for men, and blouses, skirts, and sweaters for women. There also are clothes items for boys. A wide range of styles, colors, and sizes is always available. Besides Gant, there are other famous brands in stock. The savings of 20 to 60 percent should please almost everyone.

Dexter Shoe

The Dexter shoe outlets have long been famous in New England. They feature first-quality shoes from the Dexter factory at 10 to 50 percent savings. You will find leather dress and casual styles for men and women. Older styles may be offered at even greater savings in order to make room for new styles.

Dining In

Here you will find all the necessities that make entertaining at home and dining in a pleasure. There is a good selection of china, crystal, flatware, and cookware. You will find names such as Lenox, Noritake, and Oneida, all at 20 to 50 percent off department store prices.

Distinctive Draperies

If you are shopping for custom-made draperies, check here. The Distinctive Draperies factory makes the draperies right here, using fabrics from such companies as Waverly, House 'n' Home, Fifth Avenue Designs, and J. Wolf. The selection is very large, and the savings are 33 to 50 percent.

Don-Frederick

This factory outlet features coats for everyone in the family. Wool, suede, and down coats are available here; in fact, Don-Frederick advertises itself as "the down center of New England." The assortment is excellent. Savings are 25 percent or more.

Donna Karan

Donna Karan designer collection, DKNY clothing, and accessories for ladies are offered well below retail prices.

Dooney & Bourke

Fine leather goods, accessories, and leather and fabric belts, direct from the factory. Classically styled luggage, handbags, and wallets made of water-repellent "All-Weather Leather," at good savings.

Dorr Mill Store

A tempting array of fabrics, yarns, and related items are available at irresistibly low prices. All fabrics are loomed by the Dorr Woolen Company and include solids, checks, tweeds, and plaids. Wools for suits, coats, dresses, and skirts are offered. Braiding and hooking woolens are available in a spectacular range of colors and shades.

The Calico Corner features dozens of bolts of calicoes from other manufacturers, along with a wide assortment of blankets. Both men's and women's sportswear also can be found here.

Eagle's Eye

Classic and classy women's sportswear, with savings of 30 to 50 percent off regular retail prices. Overruns and irregulars in up-to-date styles. There is also a selection of children's sportswear.

Eastern Bag and Paper Party Store

For savings of 10 to 15 percent (and even more on quantity purchases) on paper goods, be sure to stop here. You will find Scott, Jet, Comet, and Paper Art among the brand names available. Check your consumption of paper goods over a period of time; that 10 to 15 percent savings adds up.

Easy Spirit

Comfortable Easy Spirit shoes for women in casual, tailored, and dressy styles. Save 30 to 50 percent off retail prices.

Eddie Bauer

Quality clothing for the great outdoors from this respected catalog merchant and retailer. Sportswear and outerwear for men and women at up to 70 percent off original prices. A small selection of camping items and gifts.

Ellen Tracy

Misses' and petite clothing, including sportswear and the Ellen Tracy collection, at outlet prices.

Entemann's

Entemann's Bakery has been producing cakes and coffee cakes since 1898. Selections may include all-butter or chocolate loaves, Danish twists, carrot cakes, cinnamon buns, chocolate-chip cookies, and donuts. Fat-free, cholesterol-free baked goods are also available. Expect savings of 20 to 70 percent off supermarket prices due to expired or nearly expired dates on these packaged items.

Esprit

Save 30 to 70 percent off the youthful Esprit fashion lines. Misses' and children's sportswear, dresswear, shoes, and accessories.

Etienne Aigner

Women's fine shoes, handbags, and leather goods with this premier label.

E.T. Wright

Top-of-the-line men's shoes from E. T. Wright at savings from 25 to 50 percent. Most styles, including the Arch Preserver, in AA–EEE widths, sizes 7 to 14. Casual, boating, and golf shoes as well as dress models.

Exeter Handkerchief Company

When you're in need of fabric, be sure to take a look at the Handkerchief Company. You will recognize such labels as Waverly, Schumacher, John Wolf, Cyrus Clark, Pendleton, and Crompton among them. The store offers one of the widest selections of drapery and fabric remnants in New England. Savings range from 25 to 40 percent or more.

Fabrics 84

If you make your own curtains and draperies, you'll enjoy Fabrics 84, where you can save 30 to 50 percent off retail prices.

There is a good assortment of fabrics here. Be sure to bring the measurements of your windows; charts are posted for computing yardage, and the clerks are extremely helpful.

Factory Handbag Store

The Handbag Store offers a fine selection of leather handbags and small leather goods at savings of 20 to 50 percent. You will recognize Margolin, Globetrotter, Buxton, and Baronet labels among other well-known brands. On a recent visit here, we also noted a very nice group of leather jackets for sale.

Factory Party Outlet

Greeting cards at 50 percent off retail prices. Also gift wrap, accessories, and party goods at savings of 20 to 60 percent. Be sure to stock up.

Famous Brands Housewares

This is a complete kitchen store that features more than 4,000 household products: cookware, tableware, kitchen gadgets, and more. The famous brands you will recognize include Rubbermaid, Anchor Hocking, Ekco, Nordic Ware, and Mirro-Wearever, all offered at substantial savings.

Famous Footwear

Shoes for the entire family at 10 to 50 percent off department store prices. Choose from footwear by Nike, Naturalizer, Timberland, LA Gear, Keds, Reebok, Life Stride, Nunn Bush, and others.

Fanny Farmer

You'll find great candy at great prices and save 25 to 50 percent on famous chocolates, fudge, nuts, and other sorts of candy. You'll save enough to buy extra candy to nibble on your way home.

FAO Schwarz

Fine toys, dolls, stuffed animals, and educational sets from the premier Fifth Avenue toy merchant. All at savings.

Farberware

Farberware waterless cookware and accessories at good discounts.

Fieldcrest/Cannon

"Loom-to-Room" savings of 40 to 60 percent on Fieldcrest and Cannon linens for bed, bath, and table. Choose from a large selection of sheets, comforters, towels, napkins, place mats, and more, all made in the U.S.A.

Fila
Italian sportswear, men's and women's casual, golf, tennis, ski, and swim wear. Samples, seconds, overruns, and discontinued merchandise are offered at savings of 40 to 50 percent off retail.

Fire Guard
Check here for a glass fireplace enclosure unit if you are relying on your fireplace for supplemental heating. Tool sets for the fireplace are also available. Savings are 30 to 50 percent.

First Choice
First Choice sells Escada, Laurel, and Crisca upscale high fashion for women. Discounts are as high as 65 percent off designer shop prices.

Fitz and Floyd
Fitz and Floyd fine china, tableware, giftware, and home accessories at 30 to 70 percent off retail.

Florsheim
Fine men's dress and casual shoes at savings of 20 to 60 percent off retail prices.

Forecaster of Boston
Forecaster wool coats, raincoats, all-weather coats, jackets, and blazers, all at substantial savings. Classic, traditional styles in misses', petite, and half sizes.

Frederic's Mill
You'll see Garland, Pandora, Burlington, and Prego among the labels here. There is a nice assortment of sweaters, underwear, knitwear, stockings, socks, and children's pajamas. The selection of styles, sizes, and colors is certainly adequate, and the savings of 40 to 50 percent are welcome.

Frugal Fannie's
Junior, misses, and women's fashions from coats, suits, and dresses to separates and casual wear. Dozens of labels from which to choose, including Norton McNaughton, Jones New York, Ann Taylor, Adolpho,

Misty Harbor, Chaus, Land's End, WillieWear, J.H. Collectibles, and more. Large shoe department includes footwear by Joyce, Paloma, Nina, Naturalizer, Caressa, Nickels, Bandolino, and others. Expect savings of 35 to 70 percent off retail.

Fuller Brush

Stop here if the Fuller Brush man hasn't knocked at your door lately. Every conceivable kind of brush and broom is available here, along with all kinds of cleaning products. Substantial savings.

Gap

Great savings on sportswear in the unfussy Gap manner. Gap changes inventory in its retail shops every six weeks, and you reap the benefits at Gap Outlet. Sweaters, shirts, sweats, slacks, jackets, and separates in men's and misses' sizes are priced at 20 to 80 percent off retail. You'll also find Gap for Kids, Baby Gap, and some Banana Republic items.

Gardner Furniture

A full-line furniture store with outlet prices. Extensive collection of fine Nichols & Stone furniture, produced right in Gardner, Massachusetts.

Gaspar's Sausage

Manufacturers of American, Italian, and Portuguese sausage, including linguica and chourico, and other fine meat products. Mail orders taken.

Genuine Kids

Boston Traders clothing in boys' sizes 4 to 7 and 8 to 20 and in girls' sizes 4 to 6X and 7 to 14. Also infant and toddler sizes in the prestigious Boston Traders' line at up to 40 percent discounts.

Geoffrey Beene

Geoffrey Beene fine designer apparel at 20 to 50 percent off retail price tags.

George S. Preisner Pewter

An interesting collection of pewter giftware, miniatures, and jewelry will be found at this factory store. Bowls, inkwells, sugar and creamer sets, bells, and candle holders are among the stylish pewter pieces featured. Savings are 30 to 50 percent.

Giorgio Armani
Designer apparel for men and women from Giorgio Armani, Emporio Armani, and A/X Exchange. Save 30 to 70 percent on high-fashion purchases.

Gordon Shoe
Shoes for the whole family, including Bandolino, Bally, Gloria Vanderbilt, Zodiac, Candies, Capezio, Nike, Jordache, Etonic, and more. Most are the latest styles and first quality. Handbags and slippers also will be found here. Savings are 20 to 40 percent below retail.

Go>Silk
Washable silk apparel for men and women at savings up to 50 percent.

The Great American Trading Company
Old-fashioned wooden games abound, including checkers, Chinese checkers, and other nostalgic games. You can purchase a large variety of marbles by the pound, yo-yos, and even markers and checkers by the piece to replace those lost from your favorite board game. The company provides boxes for treasures such as marbles or game pieces; the small hinged or sliding-top boxes are made of balsa, cedar, or hardwood. These are good for craftspeople and collectors, as well.

Green Mountain Spinnery
The Green Mountain Spinnery sells 100 percent wool made at the spinnery and knit goods made from their yarns. For those who like the luxury of pure wool or those who enjoy knitting, this is the store. Savings range from 5 to 50 percent.

Guess? Again
Guess? jeans, loved by many, as well as other Guess? sports separates, all at substantial savings.

Gund
Famous Gund plush animals of every size and description at savings of 25 to 50 percent.

harvé benard
Stop at this outlet where America's favorite designer presents his col-

lection of high-quality clothing for men and women with discriminating tastes. The selection of career suits is outstanding. The savings are remarkable—up to 60 percent.

Hathaway/Warners/Olga
Men's dress shirts from Hathaway, Christian Dior, and Chaps by Ralph Lauren. Speedo and Nicklaus activewear, sweaters, jackets, and accessories. Also women's shirts and blouses by Lady Hathaway. This is a Warnaco outlet, so you may find other labels by this manufacturer, including intimate apparel from Olga, Warners, Blanche, and Valentino. Skiwear from White Stage, Edelweiss, and Mountain Goat. Savings of 40 to 60 percent.

HE-RO Group
Evening wear to casual wear for women from three of America's top designers: Oleg Cassini, Bill Blass, and Bob Mackie. Save 30 to 70 percent off retail.

Hickey-Freeman
Quality, well-designed suits tailored for the businessman. Also sport coats, slacks, and sportswear. Savings well below retail prices.

The Hitchcock Chair Store
The Hitchcock line of furniture is known nationwide. The factory in Riverton has been operating since 1946 and now produces upholstered furniture, wooden chairs, lamps, and giftware. In addition to the stenciled Hitchcock line, the stores also sell Madison Square, Howard Miller, Stiffel, and Baker.

Homestead Woolen Mill
A nice selection of wool and wool-blend fabrics is available at the Homestead store. Solid colors, plaids, and patterns are featured at a savings of 30 percent or more.

Howard's
Howard's features leather coats and jackets at savings of up to 40 percent. If you are looking for the classic styling and outstanding quality of

leather, you certainly will find a large number of choices here. You also will find boots, vests, gloves, handbags, briefcases, and business cases.

Hudson Paper Company
This store is well worth checking, not only for paper party goods such as plates, cups, napkins, and tablecloths, but also for regular household needs such as tissues, paper towels, and toilet tissue. Gift wrap, ribbons, and gift boxes are also here. This is a small but well-stocked store adjacent to the factory, with ample parking and helpful sales personnel. A visit here is not only thrifty, as savings are 20 percent or more, but also pleasant.

Hush Puppies
Comfortable family footwear at 25 to 75 percent off retail.

Hy-Sil Manufacturing, Gift Wrap Company of America
This gift-wrap company dates back to 1903. The factory outlet offers substantial savings on gift wraps, bows, ribbon, Christmas cards, and accessories such as gift bags and tissue paper. Note that this outlet is open only from mid-October until the holidays, so stock up while you are there.

Izod/Gant
Here you will find savings of 40 percent on Izod LaCoste and Gant sportswear for men and women. This is a good place for the persnickety shopper.

Janlynn
Needlecraft kits in floss or crewel embroidery, counted and printed cross-stitch, needlepoint, and candlewicking at 50 percent or more off retail. Kits include pillows, wall decor, garments, totes, baby items, and more.

J. C. Penney
Overstock, returns, and discontinued items from the J. C. Penney catalog, including shoes, fashions, furniture, household goods, toys, and sporting goods. A huge selection.

J. Crew

A J. Crew outlet is an upscale shop where men's and women's sportswear you have admired in the J. Crew catalog is crisply displayed: classic yet trendy shirts, sweaters, jackets, T-shirts, turtlenecks, pants, shorts, and more. All at savings to you.

Je-Mel Wood Products

You will enjoy choosing among the interesting varieties of wooden gift items in this shop. Sconces, candle holders, bowls, and other serving accessories identified as seconds by the manufacturer are featured at 33 to 40 percent off retail cost.

Jennifer Convertibles

Jennifer sleeper sofas in a variety of sizes, styles, and upholstery are offered at big savings. Some accessory pieces are available, as well.

The Jewelry Mine

The Jewelry Mine is a gold mine of attractively displayed jewelry. The store has cut gems, giving you the opportunity to choose a gem and a setting for it. The store also has attractive pewter giftware, and all prices are 30 to 40 percent under retail cost.

J. H. Collectibles

First-quality women's and petite sportswear and business apparel at 25 to 50 percent off retail.

J. K. Adams

Wooden items made by the Adams company are on display here and include ice chests, carving boards, cheese boards, knife racks, spice racks, coasters, and much more. These are offered in first- and second-quality, at 20 to 40 percent off list price. In addition, you'll find cutlery from Russel Harring, tablecloths from Mountain Weavers, and additional woodenware from Woodbury. These first-quality items are priced at 20 percent below retail.

Joan & David

Top-of-the-line Joan and David shoes for women at 30 to 50 percent savings.

Jockey

Jockey undies, tees, and sportswear for men and women at outlet prices.

John Henry and Friends

Men's and women's sportswear from John Henry, Manhattan, and Perry Ellis, with emphasis on shirts and blouses. Savings are up to 60 percent off retail prices.

Johnson Woolen Mills

In addition to its assortment of woolen blankets, Johnson offers an attractive selection of wool clothing. Jac-shirts in solids and plaids, hunting coats and pants, and chamois shirts are available for men and children. For women there are chamois shirts, coats, and capes. The selection is good, with a full range of sizes, colors, and styles offered. Savings are 10 to 25 percent. Mail-order purchases are also possible.

Johnston & Murphy

Footwear and accessories for men in a variety of elegant styles. This company has been in operation since 1850. The savings are substantial, 50 percent in some cases.

Jonathan Logan

For savings of 30 to 70 percent on women's clothing, stop here; you will find dresses, knitwear, raincoats, and sportswear from a variety of famous manufacturers. If you are looking for quality and classic styling, you will certainly find them here.

Jones New York

Classic quality business and casual wear for women at up to 70 percent off suggested retail prices.

Just Coats and Swimwear

A stock of quality coats is offered at this outlet store. Dress and sport coats for women are offered in a full range of sizes and colors. A selection of men's outerwear is also available. Look for familiar brand names such as London Fog and Liz Claiborne. Savings are 20 to 50 percent.

Keene Mill End Store

There is a good assortment of all types of fabrics to fill almost any sewing need. Related sewing accessories are also available. Adequate parking, helpful sales personnel, and savings of 20 to 40 percent round out the attractions of this store.

Kennedy Brothers Woodenware

There are hundreds of wooden items manufactured by Kennedy Brothers. If it's made of wood, it is probably here, and at savings of 25 percent on first-quality items to 50 percent or more on discontinued or second-quality items. In addition to their own woodenware, there is a complete selection of other Vermont-made and Vermont-grown products, as well as gifts and decorative items.

Large viewing windows allow you to watch the fascinating woodworking process; a slide show traces the process from tree to finished product.

Kitchen Collection/Proctor-Silex/Wearever

Cookware, bakeware, utensils, and small kitchen appliances at factory outlet prices.

Kitchen Etc.

If you are looking for any items related to the kitchen, be sure to stop here; browsing is sure to yield the right new gadget or accessory.

China, stoneware, glassware, cookware, bakeware, cutlery, gadgets, and numerous other items are here at savings of 15 to 50 percent. Names you will recognize include Noritake, Henckels, Pfaltzgraff, and Calphalon.

Kitchen Place

Utensils and all manner of kitchen and tabletop supplies can be purchased here. The brands offered at reduced prices include Anchor Hocking, Corning, Libby, Rubbermaid, Pfaltzgraff, and Wearever.

Knapp Shoe

If you are familiar with Knapp shoes, you will want to shop at this store. Here are factory-damaged and discontinued shoes at substantial savings. You may choose from dress, casual, and work shoe styles.

Knitty Gritty

This outlet offers overruns and discontinued first-quality merchandise from the mill. Sweaters in children's sizes 4 to 20, women's 32 to 40, and men's S to XL are all available in a good selection of styles and colors. The store's savings of up to 50 percent make this a worthwhile stop.

Last Straw

The Last Straw offers dozens of gift items, including baskets, wicker accessories, woodenware, and numerous other items, at savings of 20 to 50 percent.

Laura Ashley

British designer clothing for women and children, as well as linens, most in the distinctive floral prints for which Laura Ashley is noted. Also home furnishings and accessories.

Leather Loft

The Leather Loft offers a distinctive selection of small leather goods for men and women. You will enjoy the gift selections, all priced at savings of 20 to 60 percent below retail. There are jewelry boxes, attaché cases, soft luggage, handbags, wallets, belts, and more.

Leather Man, Ltd.

Belts, belts, and more belts! Some in leather, but most in casual canvas with "preppy" nautical or animal designs. Savings are 50 percent off men's, women's, and children's sizes and styles. A few handbags and small leather accessories are sold here, including a leather road-atlas holder for the person who has everything.

Leather Outpost/Buxton

Wallets, attaché cases, luggage, and portfolios by Buxton, Pierre Cardin, Swank, and others. A selection of silk neckware. Savings are 30 to 50 percent off retail.

L'eggs/Hanes/Bali

Men's, women's, and children's sizes of these recognized brands. Overstocks, closeouts, and imperfects provide savings of 20 to 50 percent on hosiery, socks, lingerie, and underwear. Why not stock up for the family? This is a good stop for back-to-school shopping.

Lenox

For elegance in table settings, Lenox certainly sets the standard. Their patterns reflect graciousness and charm and help to make dinner a very special time for family and friends. At this store you will find an extensive selection of china, crystal, and accessories at savings of 30 to 50 percent and more.

Leslie Fay

Dresses, sportswear, suits, and separates are the first reason to stop in this store. The second is the offering of skiwear and activewear for men and women.

Le Sportsac

Lightweight travel bags, handbags, and accessories for casual wear or business in a variety of shapes, sizes, and colors at 20 to 70 percent off retail.

Levine and Levine

You will find such brand names as London Fog, Misty Harbor, Jordache, Trissi, Devon, Larry Levine, totes, and Alfred Dunner. The typical savings on all items is from 20 to 50 percent.

Levi's

Wall-to-wall Levi's for men, women, and children in every conceivable waist and leg measurement. Also other Levi items, and all at outlet prices.

Libbey Glass

Libbey glassware, including stemware, barware, and party serving pieces. Crystal from L. E. Smith, dinnerware, and table accessories, all at outlet prices.

Lily of France

Lingerie, loungewear, and intimate apparel for women from Lily of France, Christian Dior, and others at savings of up to 70 percent.

Lindt of Switzerland

Fine Swiss chocolates are available at affordable prices here. Choose from Lindt truffles, assorted chocolates, bars, or holiday gift boxes.

Linens 'n Things

Whatever your linen closet might be lacking can probably be found here at savings of 20 to 40 percent. Sheets, pillowcases, towels, blankets, comforters, place mats, tablecloths, dish towels, potholders, and all related items from such major manufacturers as Dan River, Wamsutta, Cannon, and Vera are to be found in plentiful supply in the store. There's also a good selection of bedroom and bathroom furniture.

Lingerie Factory Outlet

Brand-name sleepwear, loungewear, foundations, and underwear for women from Bali, Calvin Klein, Lily of France, Lilyette, Maidenform, and Warners. Forty to 70 percent off first-quality, current selections.

Liz Claiborne

Save up to 75 percent on discontinued first-quality fashions by Liz Claiborne. You will find sportswear and dresses in misses' and petite sizes, handbags and accessories, and Claiborne menswear.

L. L. Bean Outlet

This famous mail-order house has long been synonymous with quality outdoor gear, sportswear, and clothing. Here you will find overstocks and discontinued items for the whole family; it is the merchandise you have admired in the L. L. Bean catalog, but at 50 to 80 percent off. This outlet is a must!

London Fog

London Fog rainwear, jackets, outerwear, toppers, and pant coats for men and women in a large assortment of lengths and sizes. Men's leather jackets, slacks, sport shirts, and sweaters. Also London Fog umbrellas, hats, and scarves. Savings of 50 percent.

Lorraine Mill Fabrics

One of the largest fabric stores in the country. Here you will find big savings and selection and lots of variety. If you buy fabrics, you'll love Lorraine.

Louis Hand

If you are shopping for curtains, this store is a good choice. You will find Priscilla, Cape Cod, swag, and panel curtain styles in a good selection of lengths, colors, and fabrics. Curtain hardware and draperies are also available. These items are supplemented by towels, sheets, and related accessory items. Savings are 50 percent. This is an outlet with a very courteous and helpful sales staff who make it fun to shop.

Mackintosh New England
Traditional women's outerwear manufactured in New England. Ladies' sizes in coats, jackets, and suits at savings from 30 to 70 percent. Also scarves, blankets, and a selection of women's sportswear.

Magnavox
Electronics, including audio, stereo, phones, TVs, VCRs, camcorders, and computers. Other brands are available, and everything is 25 to 60 percent off retail.

Maidenform
Intimate apparel for women, including sleepwear, lingerie, bras, and panties. Savings are often 50 to 60 percent off retail for first-quality, discontinued, and closeout merchandise.

Mainely Bags
Women's handbags (or, as some New England old-timers say, "pocketbooks") are available here in leather, pigskin, vinyl, and fabric. Also wallets and accessories at 20 to 70 percent off retail prices.

Maine State Prison Showroom
Although not a factory outlet in the usual sense of the term, this unique store is of interest to the astute shopper. You will find a variety of handcrafted items here, including furniture, nautical crafts, and unusual novelty items. The pine chopping boards are classic—and a bargain to boot.

Maine Wreath and Flower
Maine dried flowers and wreaths as well as floral wreath supplies at a savings.

Main Modes
For elegance and sophistication there's nothing that can top leather

and suede clothing. And when it's affordable, there's nothing so gratifying. Main Modes features high-quality leather and suede outerwear for men and women, at savings of approximately 60 percent. An ample variety of styles and sizes is available.

Malden Yarn Mill

Yarns and kits of the well-known Bernat Company, as well as yarns, kits, and related craft items from Bucilla, Coats & Clark, Reynolds, Unger, and other familiar names, are available here at savings from 10 to 75 percent.

Manchester Wood

Finished and unfinished furniture, including porch rockers, kitchen stools, cabinets, and occasional tables. Shaker and mission pieces, Adirondack chairs, folding tray tables, and more, all at low factory store prices.

Manhattan

Manhattan shirts and underwear, Yves Saint Laurent ties and belts, and Henry Grethel, John Henry, Valentino, and Givenchy shirts for men. For women there is Lady Manhattan, Vera, Bayard Sport, Lanvin, Amanda, and Anne Klein clothing. All items are priced at 30 to 50 percent below retail cost.

Mark Cross

Distinctive leather goods: handbags, luggage, briefcases, and wallets. Significant savings are offered from this manufacturer, which has been crafting leather since 1845.

Mark Stevens Warehouse

This is a CVS warehouse outlet.

Mary Meyer

If you are looking for a stuffed toy or doll for that special youngster in your life, here you will find dozens from which to choose. Teddies galore, plus just about any other animal you can think of, are all waiting to be new friends with that child. Savings are 20 to 50 percent at this factory store.

Micki Designer Separates

Micki-brand women's suits, separates, dresses, and accessories are offered at 50 percent off retail. This is a good stop for business attire at affordable prices.

Mikasa

Savings of up to 70 percent on first-quality dinnerware, crystal, china, giftware, flatware, cookware, and linens. Owned and operated by Mikasa.

Miltons

Fine classic sportswear and businesswear for men and women. Large selection of suits and coats from names you will recognize, all at savings of 30 to 70 percent off original Miltons' store prices.

Moda

Men's designer clothing from Calvin Klein, Giorgio Armani, Joseph Abboud, Emanual Ungaro, and others. Savings are 50 percent off retail.

Mondi

European sportswear and accessories for women with savings from 30 to 70 percent off retail.

Movado

Luxurious Swiss watches and clocks from Movado, as well as from Concord, Paiget, Corum, and Esquire. Also fine Italian leather handbags, attaché cases, and personal leather goods. Save from 25 to 75 percent.

Napier Jewelry

At the Napier factory store, fine costume jewelry is affordable because it is priced at 40 to 60 percent below retail cost. The elegant fashion jewelry featured here is considered to be closeouts of first-quality surplus stock.

Naturalizer

Ladies' dressy and casual shoes from Naturalizer and others. Comfortable savings off shoestore prices.

nautica
Nautica brand better sportswear in men's and misses' sizes. Casual wear, swimwear, and outerwear at good savings.

New Balance
Men's, women's, and children's shoes for running, walking, tennis, basketball, and cross-training. Men's and women's athletic apparel, socks, and sports bags. Twenty to 70 percent off retail prices.

New England Shoe Barn
Room after room of men's and women's designer-label sportswear, including skirts, blouses, and sweaters for women, and pants, jackets, and jeans for men. In the adjacent building are shoes and boots galore. This is just like a big department store, and the savings of 30 to 50 percent are very helpful.

9 West
Women's shoes and handbags from 9 West, Calico, and other manufacturers. Discounts up to 50 percent off retail prices.

NordicTrack
NordicTrack fitness exercisers, including skiing and walking machines, all at substantial savings.

North Country Leathers
Wallets, belts, handbags, jackets, and other leather items at discounts up to 70 percent.

North Oxford Mills
The North Oxford Mills manufactures handsome braided rugs on the premises. Many are available in colors that harmonize with most color schemes. In addition, the mills sell broadloom carpets by Galaxy and Bigelow in a lovely selection of colors and weights. Savings are 30 to 50 percent.

Nothing But 2nds
Factory seconds and closeouts from furniture manufacturers, including Yield House.

The Old Mill

The Old Mill specializes in women's sportswear at savings between 40 and 60 percent. Brand names include Country Suburbans, Weathervane, and Handmacher.

Oneida

Save 20 to 70 percent on Oneida merchandise. You will find silver trays, pitchers, bowls, and numerous other Oneida Silversmith pieces. There are stainless and silver-plated flatware, cutlery, crystal, dinnerware, and baby items. This is a great place for gift shopping.

OshKosh B'Gosh

A complete line of children's sportswear and shoes. Work wear and menswear are also sold here. This is a great place for growing young families, with discounts of 50 percent off department store prices.

Oxford Mill End

This shop offers a good assortment of yard goods, remnants, yarn, and rug material. In fact, of all the stores offering woolen remnants for rug braiding, the Mill End Store is one of the most reasonable. Their woolen yard goods are well suited to coats, skirts, slacks, and suits.

Pairpoint Glass

This shop offers an educational experience to anyone interested in glass, for here it is possible to watch the glassblowing process. The Blowing Room is open to visitors during the week. In the salesroom are handmade lead crystal vases, bowls, decanters, paperweights, candlesticks, and other gift items; savings are 30 to 50 percent.

Paper Factory

The Paper Factory outlet offers low prices on party goods and home office supplies. You will also find a nice selection of gift wrappings, decorations, balloons, and greeting cards.

Paper Warehouse

If you are in need of paper goods for party or everyday use, check the Paper Warehouse. It has a sizable selection of paper plates, cups, napkins, and related party goods. Aluminum foil, disposable baking containers, plates, and so on also are available here. Savings are 10 to 20 percent.

Parker's Candies

Sweets straight from the source. Savings on an assortment of candies suitable for gift-giving or home consumption.

Patagonia

Patagonia label clothing for men, women, and children at good savings. You will find quality discontinued items, seconds, and overruns that have that certain rugged, outdoor look.

Pepperidge Farm

Here you will find Pepperidge Farm packaged breads, rolls, cookies, crackers, snacks, and Goldfish, as well as frozen cakes, turnovers, pastries, and other Pepperidge Farms goodies. Twenty to 80 percent off retail prices, due to expired or nearly expired dates on products offered at the Thrift Stores and Outlets. Because Campbells owns Pepperidge Farms, there is a selection of Campbell soups and juices, too.

Pfaltzgraff

Pfaltzgraff stoneware in all the popular patterns, along with matching decorative pieces and table linens. Savings up to 50 percent on this made-in-the-U.S.A. tableware.

Polly Flinders

Polly Flinders dresses for girls are distinguished by their lovely, hand-smocked patterns. This classic look is offered in up-to-date styles at 40 to 60 percent savings in infant sizes through girls' 14.

Polo/Ralph Lauren

Here you will find 25 to 50 percent savings on the prestigious Polo and Ralph Lauren lines. Traditional clothing for the whole family is offered, as are the Polo/Ralph Lauren fragrances, leather goods, footwear, accessories, and selected home furnishings. Nothing is being given away here, but you will find the prices for Polo lower than those at a department store or specialty store.

Prestige Fragrance and Cosmetics

Well-known men's and women's fragrances, toiletries, and cosmetics, including Calvin Klein and Yves St. Laurent, sell at 25 to 70 percent savings. The makeup-counter staff provides department store service at outlet prices.

Pro Golf Discount
Pro Golf offers all the items a golfer ever needs, from clubs (including those for left-handed people) to golfing umbrellas to appropriate clothing. Savings are 20 to 40 percent.

Providence Yarn
This is New England's largest display of hand-knitting yarns and accessories at mill prices. A great stop if you are into knitting. And to make carrying your knitting with you even easier, enjoy the complete line of luggage, totes, and sport bags at 30 to 75 percent off retail prices.

Putamayo
This outlet is a real find for gals. Putamayo dresses, sportswear, and accessories (many in distinctive batiks) are offered at substantial savings off department and specialty store prices.

Reebok/Rockport
Reebok athletic shoes and apparel—including the Weebok line for kids—and Rockport walking shoes for men and women at substantial savings.

Reed and Barton Silversmiths
This store is located in the factory. Choose from Reed and Barton sterling, silver plate, pewter, stainless, brass, and crystal, all at factory-direct prices. Also savings on fourteen-karat gold and sterling silver jewelry. This is a great stop for gift shopping.

Ribbon Outlet
Ribbon Outlet offers a splendid selection of 2,500 ribbons and trims. You can buy whole spools, by the yard, or in precut lengths. Craft supplies and bridal and seasonal items will help you complete your projects. Savings are up to 50 percent.

Rockport Shoe
Engineered in the 1970s, Rockport shoes are the epitome of walking

shoes, "shoes that make you feel like walking." Men's and women's sizes for fitness and hiking activities, as well as comfortable casual, dress, and sandal styles. Savings of 20 to 50 percent.

Royal Doulton

A delightful shop designed like a fine retail store. If you are looking for a baby gift, what could be better than a Royal Doulton double-handled mug, feeding dish, or other china piece? If you are looking for a wedding gift, there are all the Royal Doulton china patterns, crystal, or other accessory items. For a special occasion there are Royal Doulton figurines, toby mugs, or Royal Albert items. You'll find that the savings of 30 to 70 percent make this a very practical choice.

R. Smith Furniture

The R. Smith Furniture Outlet offers savings of 25 to 40 percent on a selection of traditional and colonial furniture. You will find Temple Stuart, Bassett, La-Z-Boy, Hale, and many other brands at this store.

Rug Factory

For years we have been calling this a delightful store, where customers are genuinely welcome. It continues to be a great place to shop for braided rugs.

Russell Stover

Here you will find the Russell Stover Candies your sweet tooth has come to crave and enjoy. Quality Russell Stover chocolates, jellies, and other assortments are offered at excellent savings. The boxed selections make nice gifts.

Saks Fifth Avenue Clearinghouse

Designer clothing for men and women from the racks of this well-known New York retailer at 30 to 70 percent off original prices. Saks Private Label, too.

Samsonite

Save up to 60 percent on Samsonite and Lark samples, overstocks, and discontinued items. A great stop for your luggage needs.

Samuel Robert

If you're looking for sophisticated apparel, Samuel Robert is a must. The ultrasuede garments here exude self-confidence, and there are perfectly coordinated accessory items.

Sandpiper Creations

Sandpiper's outdoor furniture is maintenance-free pipe furniture, designed for porch, patio, pool, or yacht use. Its contemporary styling is very attractive, and the quality construction should provide years of use. The company also manufactures Pied Piper furniture for children.

Savings at the outlet store are 50 percent below retail. We have personally enjoyed this quality outdoor furniture at home.

Saucony Soft-Bilt Athletic Shoes

High-quality performance shoes for men and women for running, walking, tennis, aerobics, basketball, and other sports. Savings up to 50 percent.

Saxony Coat

If names such as London Fog, Misty Harbor, harvé benard, Junior Gallery, Bromleigh, and Sassoon entice you, you'll be pleased with a shopping expedition to Saxony Coat Company. The store offers these brand names at savings of 25 to 40 percent.

Seaport Fabric

First-quality merchandise and seconds from Mario Buatta, Schumacher, Waverly, and other fine manufacturers of fabric. A great selection at savings from 30 to 70 percent.

Seiko

Watches, wall clocks, desk clocks, and travel clocks from Seiko, Pulsar, Lassale, Lorus, and Jaz-Paris. All at outlet prices.

Slater Fabrics

First-quality fabrics for home furnishings and fashions for women and children. Most designs available in large quantities—just the thing for coordinating a room or a children's group or choir. Most fabrics are available at an economical $1.25 per yard. It's such a great savings that you can't afford not to shop here.

Socks Galore and More

Floor-to-ceiling displays of socks for men, women, and children fill this store. Sport, casual, and dress styles sell at 40 to 50 percent off retail, with extra savings for quantity purchases. Mail order is available. If you have thrown away your darning needle, this is a good place to replace those worn-out socks.

Sox Market

Name-brand socks and hosiery for men, women, and children at discount prices.

Spaulding & Frost

Spaulding & Frost has been making wooden barrels and tubs since 1870. Their business is in a very interesting, hundred-year-old building. You're sure to enjoy the building, but you're even more likely to wonder at their products. Ice buckets, keg stools, planters, hampers, magazine buckets, sewing buckets, even rain barrels—these are just a few of the many items offered in the basic barrel design. Firsts, seconds, irregulars, and rejects are offered, with savings ranging from 30 to 65 percent.

Stetson Hat

Western, dress, and sport hats as well as cuffey caps are offered here; the special Stetson style is clearly the drawing card for the man or woman who is conscious of style. Savings are about 15 to 20 percent on first-quality merchandise and up to 50 percent on factory irregulars.

Stitchers

Curtains manufactured on the spot by the third generation of the family that created the nationally famous Cape Cod–style curtains and the newer Victorian full-size swags. Bring in a list of measurements, swatches, and wallpaper samples. The staff will help you choose the right fabrics and offer advice.

Stride Rite/Keds/Sperry-Topsider

Footwear for the entire family from Stride Rite, Keds, and Sperry-Topsider at savings from 20 to 50 percent.

Sudberry House

Sudberry House makes wooden accessories for needlework, such as footstools, trays, and game boards. They also sell needlework kits to fit their wooden items. The atmosphere is distinctly friendly and helpful, and the savings are 50 percent; if you enjoy needlework, put this store on your not-to-be-missed list.

Sunglass Outlet

Sunglasses from top manufacturers including Carrerra, Ray-Ban, and Vuarnet, all at terrific savings.

Swank

This is a good source for swanky, small leather goods, travel bags and accessories, jewelry, and men's ties. Anne Klein, Pierre Cardin, Royal Copenhagen, and Swank are displayed at discounts from 50 to 80 percent off retail.

Sweatertown U.S.A.

If you are shopping for sweaters, you will want to check out the selection here. You will find Northern Isles, Kenneth Too, and Prego among the available brands. The excellent selection and the helpful savings of 30 percent combine to make this a good shopping choice.

Talbots

Overstocks of classy Talbots classics come home to the outlet store at the end of the season. The dressy dresses, suits, tailored outfits, and sportswear you have admired at one of Talbots's 180 shops or in the Talbots catalog may be found here. Save 20 to 90 percent off retail on petite and misses' sizes 2 to 20. Accessories, lingerie, and ladies' shoes, as well as a selection of Talbots for boys' and girls' clothing to size 14.

Tanner

Tanner, Tanner Country, and Tanner Sport ladies' classic apparel at 25 to 80 percent off retail prices.

Textile Warehouse

You will find closeouts, special purchases, and first quality and slightly irregular famous-maker towels at this outlet. Some of the towels are even sold by the pound! There are comforters, pillows, and enough sheets to guarantee sweet dreams for years to come. You'll also find factory-direct fabrics—knits, velour, sweatshirt fabrics, spandex, and rubgy cottons.

Thompson Candy Store

This store is heaven for chocolate lovers. Candy novelties for holidays and special occasions, as well as a variety of chocolates by the pound, are featured here, all at savings of 20 to 25 percent. If you're on a diet, you'd better not stop here, because you won't be able to resist these delicious candies.

Three D Bed and Bath

Here you will find a great selection of better towels, sheets, comforters, pillows, shower curtains, and lots of accessories, all pleasantly displayed. Some tasteful kitchen items are available as well. If you are redoing a bedroom or bath or are just plain tired of your sheets and towels, this is a good stop.

Timberland

If you are looking for quality outdoor footwear, you will find it at Timberland; by shopping at the factory store, you will save 40 percent to boot.

Factory seconds of Timberland boots and shoes are here. You will find rugged 6-inch and 10-inch boots, hiking and trail shoes, boat shoes, pac-boots, casual oxfords, chukkas, and the traditional penny loafers.

Tinsel Town/Patioland

Trees, garlands, icicles, wreaths, and a selection of craft items are arrayed at savings of up to 50 percent. You will also find a line of summer furniture and accessories at factory outlet prices.

Top of the Line Cosmetics and Fragrances

You can afford to treat yourself to your favorite fragrances and cosmetics when you shop at Top of the Line. There is a large selection of items from many well-known producers. You will see Halston, Calvin Klein, Germaine Monteil, and fifty other nationally known brands at this outlet. Savings are 35 to 75 percent.

totes

Tote that barge! Lift that umbrella! Stop at this outlet if you're interested in saving money on a variety of accessories designed to make your life a whole lot easier—and drier. You'll find the aforementioned umbrellas plus raincoats, jackets, headwear for men and women, luggage, scarves, and more.

Townshend Furniture

You will be impressed with the selection of traditional furniture in this factory store. It is all well constructed and beautifully finished. Sofas, chairs, tables, hutches, coffee tables, chests, desks, end tables, and accessory items are found here at prices that are kind to your budget. If you are looking for that piece of furniture to add the perfect finishing touch to your room, or if you're just starting out, this is a good place to shop.

Toys Unlimited

Toys and games from Hasbro, Tonka, Mattel, Milton Bradley, Fisher-Price, Playskool, Matchbox, Parker Brothers, and more. Savings from 40 to 70 percent.

Trina

Trina manufactures a nice collection of cosmetic kits, travel kits, carry-on luggage, Genie evening and straw handbags, and boutique gift items. They even have a line of baby bedding with coordinated bags. The merchandise consists of closeouts, discontinued styles, samples, and seconds. Savings are 30 to 50 percent or more. This is a good place to shop for gift items and your own needs. It is a favorite of ours.

TSE Cashmere

Cashmere sweaters for men and women at 30 percent off retail prices.

Turfer Jacket

You'll find an array of jackets for your team of outlet shoppers—or, more traditionally, sports teams from school or work. Nylon, corduroy, wool, and polar fleece are some of the materials used. You'll also find sweats, jackets, and coats for the entire family at 20 to 50 percent off retail.

Twin-Kee Clothing

Bring the family to Twin-Kee to shop for all-weather coats. There is an impressive selection from which to choose, and the savings are approximately 30 percent.

Two's Company

Screen-printed T-shirts, sweatshirts, golf shirts, baseball hats, visors, and more. Several Rhode Island, Newport, and Cape Cod designs to choose from, in addition to more than a hundred other popular designs. Custom printing available.

Uxbridge Yarn Mill

Bernat Company yarns and kits are one of the exciting items found here. Perfect for people who like to work with their hands. You will also find yarns, kits, and related craft items from Bucilla, Coats & Clark, Reynolds, Unger, and other familiar names with savings from 10 to 75 percent.

Van Heusen

Owned and operated by the Van Heusen Company, this outlet carries a huge selection of current-season, first-quality men's and women's apparel with Van Heusen, Lady Van Heusen, and designer-brand labels at a savings ranging from 30 to 60 percent.

Vermont Wood Specialties

Seconds of wooden giftware manufactured in this factory include cheese boards, lazy Susans, condiment sets, ice buckets, and bowls. The selection is large and varied, and savings of 40 percent are offered. The store also carries Aremetale, Mary Meyer items, and Vermont maple syrup and candy.

Veryfine

Juices galore, from cases of 10-ounce bottles to supersize 128-ounce jugs. You will find apple, grape, orange, cranberry, grapefruit, and pineapple juices, as well as punch, lemonade, and tea. Veryfine's Chillers and Apple Quenchers may include exotic combinations such as apple/peach/kiwi or apple/black cherry/white grape. Stock up your pantry at savings up to 80 percent off supermarket prices.

V.F. Outlet
Recognize the initials? This is the Vanity Fair factory outlet, so you can plan to find many well-known brands here in styles for men, women, and children. The extensive merchandise available should offer something to please everyone, and the values are excellent.

Villeroy & Boch
Villeroy & Boch are prestigious manufacturers of fine European china, crystal, and bakeware. This store offers enticing savings of 40 to 70 percent on their seconds and discontinued merchandise. There is also a Hartmann boutique carrying luggage, garment bags, briefcases, and more.

Wallet Works
This factory-owned- and -operated store features savings on more than 150 different styles of men's and women's leather wallets. You'll find luggage, handbags, briefcases, and travel gifts. Savings range from 25 to 75 percent.

Ware Sports Wear
Manufacturer's outlet for top-notch private labels for women, including Blyle, Castleberry, Carroll Reed, and Talbots. Substantial savings.

Waring
Who hasn't heard of a Waring Blendor™? Waring appliances have always had a fine reputation. At the factory you can purchase their small appliances at savings of 50 percent or more. Blenders, blender accessories, electric mixers, food steamers, food processors, and more are to be found in all the Waring colors. Special closeout items are sometimes featured.

Warnaco
A tremendous selection of clothing for men, women, and children is available, with excellent choices of sizes, styles, and colors. With items ranging from lingerie for women to jackets for men, the store is an outstanding asset to everyone's clothing budget.

Brand names to expect here include White Stag, Warner's, SW1, Spalding, Christian Dior, Edelweiss, Hathaway, Speedo, Pringle, Puritan, Thane, Day's, Hirsch Weis, Chaps by Ralph Lauren, Austin, and Destino/Dior.

Warren of Stafford
If you sew, plan a trip here. The selection offered by this prestigious woolen mill is outstanding, with cashmere and camel hair featured at very desirable prices. A lovely wardrobe of suits, skirts, blazers, and slacks could be sewn from these luxury fabrics; savings amount to 60 percent or more. In addition, coordinated linens, cotton, and silks are in stock.

Waterford/Wedgwood
Elegant Waterford crystal from Ireland, as well as Wedgwood, Johnson Brothers, Ainsley, and Franciscan fine dinnerware and giftware, are offered here at substantial savings off department store prices. This is a wonderful spot to complete place settings of crystal and china or to buy wedding or anniversary gifts.

WearGuard
Rugged work clothes for the hardworking man or woman. Outerwear, shirts, pants, and more come directly from the WearGuard factory in the same building. Also available are non-uniform-looking uniforms for the medical professional, and clothing, aprons, and toques for the restaurant/catering trade. A selection of serviceable shoes (and racks of monogrammed sample jackets—"Joe" from "Queen City Tree Topping," for example) rounds out the offerings here.

Welcome Home
For the person into country decor, Cape Craft offers housewares at 30 to 50 percent off retail. Included in the inventory are framed prints, brassware, rugs and throws, woodenware, table linens, porcelain dolls, candles, giftware, and more.

Wellington Curtain
The Wellington store offers curtains, draperies, or bedspreads and more household accessories, all at savings of 20 to 40 percent. The wide range of sizes, styles, and colors will give you lots from which to choose.

Weston Bowl Mill and Annex
Weston is an attractive Vermont town, and the Bowl Mill and Annex is a fun place to visit. The mill makes an almost overwhelming variety of quality woodenware on the premises, and there is something for everyone here.

Westport, Ltd.
At Westport, Ltd., you'll find clothes for the career woman with a sense of classic style that spells success. Look for Westport, Ltd.; Princeton Club; Atrium; and Milano Design Group labels. The outlet stocks a selection of suits, dresses, sportswear, and separates in sizes 4 to 14.

West Rindge Baskets
Here are authentic, made–in–New England ash baskets, the perfect souvenir of your New England vacation or a great gift for a friend. A variety of basket types in firsts and seconds is offered at savings of 20 to 50 percent. Be sure to watch the baskets being made, an interesting craft that has changed little over the years.

Whiting and Davis
Whiting and Davis offers its elegant line of gold mesh evening handbags, purse accessories, fashion accessories, and costume jewelry at savings of 40 to 70 percent. (Whiting and Davis, by the way, is the oldest handbag factory in the United States.)

Winchendon Furniture
If you are shopping for furniture or decorative accessory items such as lamps, you will find an extensive selection here at savings of 30 percent. You can choose from brands such as Thomasville, Conover, Leather Craft, Hardon, Stiffel, Wildwood, and King Koil. Inquire about the Warehouse Bargain Annex, which offers damaged and discontinued merchandise at proportionate savings.

Woodbury's of Shelburne
If you are looking for very attractive woodenware, you will want to stop here. Woodbury's offers hand-turned salad bowls, trays, lazy Susans, compotes, trivets, and other accessory items. Both firsts and selected seconds are available at savings of 20 to 30 percent.

Worcester Tool

For 100 years the Walden Wrench factory has been at this location, manufacturing tools and wrenches popular with handypersons. The factory store is right in the factory, offering 50 percent savings. The store supplements its line with hand and power tools from other manufacturers. You'll find Rockwell Delta woodworking machines, Black & Decker, Bosch, Stanley, Milwaukee, and more, all at a savings.

World Wide Games

Imported games, board games, kites, Legos, and Nintendo games are to be found here at outlet prices. Also craft supplies galore for the craftsperson, parent, teacher, or child.

WorleyBeds

WorleyBeds has an extensive selection of all types of bedroom furniture, including waterbeds, electric beds, bunk beds, brass beds, sleeper sofas, mattresses, and box springs. Special-size bedding can be made to order here. In addition to their own brand, they carry Comfortron AdjustaBeds, Dresher Brass, Koehler, Schjeiger, and other well-known names in the field of bedroom furniture, all at savings of 30 to 50 percent; savings on the Worley line are 60 percent.

Yankee Candle

As you open the door, the fragrances welcome you and the sight of the attractively displayed candles and gift items manufactured by Yankee Candle Company delights you. You will find a varying selection of seconds in addition to the first-quality merchandise. Expect to save 30 to 50 percent on these items.

Yield House

New England colonial furniture and home accessories at 30 to 50 percent off retail. Included in the inventory are overruns, discontinued pieces, and damaged items. All sales are final.

Connecticut

Numbers at the left of this legend correspond to the numbers on the accompanying map. The number to the right of each city's or town's name is the page number on which that municipality's outlets first appear in this book.

1. Branford, 49
2. Bridgeport, 50
3. Brookfield, 51
4. Colchester, 51
5. Danbury, 52
6. Deep River, 53
7. East Windsor, 53
8. Essex, 53
9. Farmington, 54
10. Glastonbury, 55
11. Groton, 55
12. Hamden, 56
13. Lisbon, 56
14. Madison, 57
15. Manchester, 58
16. Meriden, 58
17. Milford, 59
18. Monroe, 60
19. Mystic, 60

20. New Hartford, 62
21. New London, 62
22. Newtown, 62
23. North Haven, 63
24. Norwalk, 63
25. Norwich, 66
26. Old Lyme, 67
27. Orange, 68
28. Putnam, 68
29. Riverton, 69
30. Southport, 69
31. Stafford Springs, 70
32. Stamford, 70
33. Stratford, 70
34. Wallingford, 71
35. Waterbury, 71
36. Westport, 72
37. Woodbury, 72

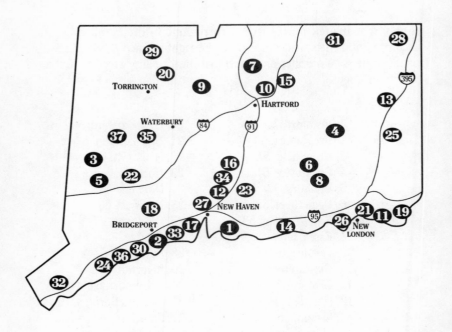

Branford

Branford Outlet Center
249–251 West Main Street
Boston Post Road (Route 1)

Directions: From I–95 North take exit 51 (Frontage Road); follow right off exit ramp onto Route 1 for approximately 2 miles.
Phone: (203) 483–0729
Hours: 10:00 A.M.–6:00 P.M., Monday–Wednesday and Saturday; 10:00 A.M.–9:00 P.M., Thursday–Friday; noon–5:00 P.M., Sunday
Handicapped Accessible: Yes
Restaurants: Grandma Lee's Eating Place in complex; Arby's, Friendly's, McDonald's nearby on Route 1
Attractions: There's a trolley museum in Branford; Yale University campus and its art galleries are in nearby New Haven.

Outlets:
Aileen
American Tourister
Banister Shoe
Bass
Champion/Hanes
Izod/Gant
Jennifer Convertibles
Jones New York
Just Coats and Swimwear
Kitchen Place
Leather Loft
L'eggs/Bali/Hanes
Prestige Fragrance and Cosmetics
Three D Bed and Bath
Van Heusen
Welcome Home

Bridgeport

The Barn of Lieff
50 Hurd Avenue

Directions: Exit 27A off I–95 to Hurd Avenue.
Phone: (203) 334–3396
Hours: 10:00 A.M.–5:00 P.M., Monday–Saturday; noon–4:00 P.M., Sunday
Credit Cards: MasterCard, Visa
Personal Checks: Yes, with proper identification
Handicapped Accessible: Yes
Restaurants: McDonald's
Bus Tours: Yes

Eastern Bag and Paper Party Store
459 Iranistan Avenue

Directions: Exit 26 off I–95 South or exit 26 off I–95 North.
Phone: (203) 334–4111; (800) 243–4447
Hours: 9:00 A.M.–6:00 P.M., Monday–Friday; 9:00 A.M.–5:00 P.M., Saturday, closed Sundays
Credit Cards: MasterCard, Visa
Personal Checks: Yes, with proper identification
Bus Tours: No

Main Modes
1225 Connecticut Avenue

Directions: Exit 31 off I–95 to Route 1, left onto Stratford Avenue to Connecticut Avenue.
Phone: (203) 366–3565
Hours: 10:00 A.M.–3:00 P.M., Sunday–Friday
Credit Cards: American Express, Discover, MasterCard, Visa
Personal Checks: Yes, with proper identification
Handicapped Accessible: No
Bus Tours: Yes

Warnaco
130 Gregory Street

Directions: Take exit 27 off I–95. Go south on Lafayette Boulevard to Gregory Street. Turn right onto Gregory Street.
Phone: (203) 579–8164
Hours: 9:30 A.M.–5:30 P.M., Monday–Saturday; noon–5:00 P.M., Sunday
Credit Cards: Discover, MasterCard, Visa
Personal Checks: Yes, with proper identification
Handicapped Accessible: Yes
Bus Tours: Yes

Brookfield

Stetson Hat
#1 Grays Bridge Common

Directions: I–84 to exit 7 North, Federal Road exit. Take right on Federal Road.
Phone: (203) 740–1777
Hours: 9:00 A.M.–5:00 P.M., Monday–Saturday
Credit Cards: Discover, MasterCard, Visa
Personal Checks: Yes, with proper identification
Handicapped Accessible: Yes
Bus Tours: Yes

Colchester

Levine and Levine
120 Lebanon Avenue

Directions: Route 2 to exit 18 toward Lebanon.
Phone: (203) 537–2373, or 537–2374
Hours: 10:00 A.M.–6:00 P.M., Monday–Wednesday and Friday; 10:00 A.M.–8:00 P.M., Thursday; 10:00 A.M.–5:00 P.M., Saturday–Sunday

Credit Cards: Discover, MasterCard, Visa
Personal Checks: Yes, with proper identification
Handicapped Accessible: Yes
Restaurants: Colchester Bakery next door

World Wide Games
Mill Street

Directions: From Route 2 East take exit 18 to Lebanon.
Phone: (203) 537–2325; (800) 243–9232, ext. 262
Hours: 9:00 A.M.–5:00 P.M., Wednesday–Friday; 10:00 A.M.–4:00 P.M., Saturday; closed Sunday and Tuesday
Credit Cards: American Express, MasterCard, Visa
Personal Checks: Yes, with proper identification
Restaurants: Colchester Bakery has wonderful breads and pastries.

Danbury

Pepperidge Farm
Danbury Square Shopping Center
15 Backus Avenue, Unit 3

Directions: Call ahead.
Phone: (203) 797–1718
Hours: 9:30 A.M.–6:00 P.M., Monday–Friday; 9:30 A.M.–5:00 P.M., Saturday; noon–5:00 P.M., Sunday
Credit Cards: No
Personal Checks: Yes, United States, with proper identification
Handicapped Accessible: Yes
Bus Tours: Yes

Deep River

The Great American Trading Company
39 Main Street

Directions: Route 9 to exit 5 to center of Deep River. Turn left on Main Street. Outlet is ½ mile on right.
Phone: (203) 526–4335
Hours: 10:00 A.M.–5:00 P.M., Monday–Sunday
Credit Cards: MasterCard, Visa on purchase of $20 or more
Personal Checks: Yes, with proper identification
Attractions: Not far from Essex or the charming village of Chester.

East Windsor

Cohoes, Ltd.
Route 5

Directions: I–91 to exit 45 to Route 5 North.
Phone: (203) 623–2591
Hours: 10:00 A.M.–9:00 P.M., Monday–Friday; 10:00 A.M.–6:00 P.M., Saturday; noon–5:00 P.M., Sunday
Credit Cards: MasterCard, Visa
Personal Checks: Yes, with proper identification
Handicapped Accessible: Yes

Essex

Leather Man, Ltd.
Essex Industrial Park

Directions: Route 9 to exit 3 to Route 153 West; turn right on Bokum Road; outlet is on right.
Phone: (203) 767–8231; out of state (800) 243–6681

Hours: 8:00 A.M.–4:00 P.M., Monday–Friday
Credit Cards: No
Personal Checks: Yes, with proper identification
Handicapped Accessible: Yes
Attractions: Not far from the Essex Steam Train.

Van Heusen
3 Main Street

Directions: Route 9 to exit 3 East to center of Essex; outlet is on the left as you enter Main Street.
Phone: (203) 767–0870
Hours: 9:00 A.M.–6:00 P.M., Monday–Saturday; noon–6:00 P.M., Sunday
Credit Cards: Discover, MasterCard, Visa
Personal Checks: Yes, with proper identification
Handicapped Accessible: Yes
Attractions: The Connecticut River Museum is at the foot of Main Street.

Farmington

Pepperidge Farm
Loehmann's Plaza
230 Farmington Avenue

Directions: Call ahead
Phone: (203) 677–5805
Hours: 9:00 A.M.–5:30 P.M., Monday–Saturday; 11:30 A.M.–4:00 P.M., Sunday
Credit Cards: No
Personal Checks: Yes, United States, with proper identification
Handicapped Accessible: Yes
Bus Tours: Yes

Glastonbury

Pepperidge Farm
Griswold Mall
2862 Main Street

Directions: Call ahead.
Phone: (203) 659–1424
Hours: 9:30 A.M.–5:30 P.M., Monday–Saturday; 11:00 A.M.–4:00 P.M., Sunday
Credit Cards: No
Personal Checks: Yes, United States, with proper identification
Handicapped Accessible: Yes
Bus Tours: Yes

Groton

Arrow Paper Party Store
84 Plaza Court
Groton Shopping Plaza

Directions: Take I–95 to exit 85. Follow Route 1 North for approximately 1 mile.
Phone: (203) 445–1165
Hours: 9:00 A.M.–6:00 P.M., Monday–Wednesday and Friday; 9:00 A.M.–8:00 P.M., Thursday; 9:00 A.M.–5:00 P.M., Saturday; 10:00 A.M.–4:00 P.M., Sunday
Credit Cards: Discover, MasterCard, Visa
Personal Checks: Yes, with proper identification
Handicapped Accessible: Yes
Bus Tours: Yes

Hamden

Pepperidge Farm
3000 Whitney Avenue

Directions: Call ahead.
Phone: (203) 288–3301
Hours: 9:30 A.M.–6:00 P.M., Monday–Friday; 9:30 A.M.–5:00 P.M., Saturday; 11:00 A.M.–3:00 P.M., Sunday
Credit Cards: No
Personal Checks: Yes, United States, with proper identification
Handicapped Accessible: Yes
Bus Tours: No

Saxony Coat
1443 Dixwell Avenue

Directions: Route 15 North to exit 60.
Phone: (203) 288–3600
Hours: 10:00 A.M.–5:30 P.M., Monday–Saturday; 10:00 A.M.–9:00 P.M., Thursday; noon–5:00 P.M., Sunday (closed Thursday evening and Sunday during summer)
Credit Cards: MasterCard, Visa
Personal Checks: Yes, with proper identification
Handicapped Accessible: Yes
Bus Tours: Yes

Lisbon

Fabrics 84
Route 12

Directions: Exit 84 off Route 395.
Phone: (203) 376–4441
Hours: 9:00 A.M.–3:45 P.M., Monday–Saturday
Credit Cards: No

Personal Checks: Yes, with proper identification
Handicapped Accessible: Yes
Bus Tours: Yes

Madison

Arrow Paper Party Store
102 Wall Street

Directions: From I–95 South take exit 61. At end of ramp, turn left. At second light, turn left and continue to end of street. From I–95 North take exit 61. Turn right at end of ramp. At second light, turn left and continue to end of street.
Phone: (203) 245–0645
Hours: 9:00 A.M.–6:00 P.M., Monday–Friday; 9:00 A.M.–5:00 P.M., Saturday; closed Sunday
Credit Cards: Discover, MasterCard, Visa
Personal Checks: Yes, with proper identification
Handicapped Accessible: No
Bus Tours: Yes

Pepperidge Farm
200 Boston Post Road (Route 1)

Directions: Call ahead.
Phone: (203) 245–3274
Hours: 9:30 A.M.–6:00 P.M., Monday–Friday; 9:30 A.M.–5:00 P.M., Saturday; noon–5:00 P.M., Sunday
Credit Cards: No
Personal Checks: Yes, United States, with proper identification
Handicapped Accessible: Yes
Bus Tours: Yes

Manchester

J. C. Penney
1360 Tolland Turnpike

Directions: I–84 to exit 62.
Phone: (203) 647–1143
Hours: 9:00 A.M.–9:30 P.M. Monday–Saturday; 10:00 A.M.–6:00 P.M. Sunday
Features: Located in the New England J. C. Penney Catalog Distribution Center
Credit Cards: American Express, J. C. Penney, MasterCard, Visa
Personal Checks: Yes, with proper identification
Handicapped Accessible: Yes

Meriden

Connecticut Gift
1247 East Main Street

Directions: East Main Street exit off I–91; turn left to the store.
Phone: (203) 237–0429
Hours: 9:30 A.M.–5:30 P.M., Monday, Wednesday, Friday, and Saturday; 9:30 A.M.–9:00 P.M., Tuesday and Thursday; noon–5:00 P.M., Sunday in November and December only
Credit Cards: MasterCard, Visa
Personal Checks: Yes, with proper identification
Handicapped Accessible: Yes
Bus Tours: Yes

Napier Jewelry
1231 East Main Street, in Meriden Parkade

Directions: I–91 to East Main Street exit. Head east on East Main Street. Meriden Parkade is on the right.
Phone: (203) 238–3087

Hours: 10:00 A.M.–6:00 P.M., Monday–Wednesday and Saturday; 10:00 A.M.–8:00 P.M., Thursday–Friday
Credit Cards: Discover, MasterCard, Visa
Personal Checks: Yes, with proper identification
Handicapped Accessible: Yes
Bus Tours: Yes

Thompson Candy
80 South Vine Street

Directions: East Main Street exit off I–91 to West Main; left onto South Vine Street.
Phone: (203) 235–2541
Hours: 9:00 A.M.–5:00 P.M., Monday–Friday
Credit Cards: No
Personal Checks: Yes, with proper identification
Handicapped Accessible: No
Restaurants: McDonald's
Bus Tours: Yes

Milford

Eastern Bag and Paper Party Store
200 Research Drive

Directions: Take exit 40 from I–95.
Phone: (800) 243–4447
Hours: 8:30 A.M.–5:15 P.M., Monday–Friday; 9:00 A.M.–5:00 P.M., Saturday
Credit Cards: MasterCard, Visa
Personal Checks: Yes, with proper identification
Bus Tours: No

Monroe

Hudson Paper Company
Clock Tower Shopping Center
Route 25

Direction: Take exit 49 off the Merritt Parkway and head north on Route 25.
Phone: (203) 261-3701
Hours: 9:00 A.M.–5:30 P.M., Monday–Saturday
Credit Cards: American Express, MasterCard, Visa
Personal Checks: Yes, with proper identification
Handicapped Accessible: Yes
Bus Tours: Yes

Mystic

Mystic Factory Outlets I & II
12 Coogan Boulevard

Directions: I–95 to exit 90; south on Route 27 to traffic light at Coogan Boulevard; take left up hill ¼ mile to MFO on right.
Phone: (203) 443-4788
Hours: 10:00 A.M.–9:00 P.M., Monday–Friday; 10:00 A.M.–6:00 P.M., Saturday; noon–5:00 P.M., Sunday; extended holiday hours
Handicapped Accessible: Yes
Restaurants: Chinese restaurant in complex; McDonald's and Friendly's on Route 27; and Mystic Pizza, Bee Bee Dairy, and other restaurants between the outlets and town
Bus Tours: Yes
Attractions: Mystic Aquarium is just north of the outlets; Mystick Village, a complex of retail shops, is across the street; Mystic Seaport is a nationally known "living history" reconstruction of a seaport town.

Outlets:
MFO I:
Aileen
Cape Isle Knitters
L'eggs/Bali/Hanes
Manhattan
Prestige Fragrance and Cosmetics
Ribbon Outlet
Swank
Van Heusen
MFO II:
Banister Shoe
Bass
Champion/Hanes
Corning/Revere
Famous Brands Housewares
Geoffrey Beene
Izod/Gant
London Fog
Polly Flinders
Socks Galore and More

Seaport Fabric
Greenmanville Avenue (Route 27)

Directions: I–95 to exit 90; south on Route 27; store is on left.
Phone: (203) 536–8668
Hours: 9:30 A.M.–5:00 P.M., Monday–Saturday
Credit Cards: MasterCard, Visa
Personal Checks: Yes, with proper identification
Handicapped Accessible: Yes
Bus Tours: No

New Hartford

Waring
Route 44

Directions: Route 44 between Canton and New Hartford Center.
Phone: (203) 379–0731
Hours: 10:00 A.M.–3:00 P.M., Monday–Friday
Credit Cards: MasterCard, Visa
Personal Checks: Yes, with proper identification

New London

Arrow Paper Party Store
567 Colman Street

Directions: Exit 82 off I–95. Left at end of ramp, then past two traffic lights to store on left.
Phone: (203) 447–3350
Hours: 9:00 A.M.–6:00 P.M., Monday–Friday; 9:00 A.M.–5:00 P.M., Saturday; 10:00 A.M.–2:00 P.M., Sunday
Credit Cards: Discover, MasterCard, Visa
Personal Checks: Yes, with proper identification
Handicapped Accessible: Yes
Bus Tours: Yes

Newtown

Pepperidge Farm
150 South Main Street

Directions: Call ahead.
Phone: (203) 426–4200
Hours: 9:30 A.M.–8:00 P.M., Monday–Friday; 9:30 A.M.–5:00 P.M., Saturday; 11:00 A.M.–5:00 P.M., Sunday

Credit Cards: No
Personal Checks: Yes, United States, with proper identification
Handicapped Accessible: Yes
Bus Tours: No

North Haven

Fire Guard
352 Sackett Point Road

Directions: Exit 9 off I–91.
Phone: (203) 248–9308
Hours: 10:00 A.M.–6:00 P.M., Monday–Saturday; 11:00 A.M.–3:00 P.M., Sunday
Credit Cards: MasterCard, Visa
Personal Checks: Yes, with proper identification
Handicapped Accessible: No
Bus Tours: Yes

Norwalk

Genuine Kids
Empire Plaza
650 West Avenue

Directions: Exit 15 off I–95.
Phone: (203) 855–1401
Hours: 9:30 A.M.–6:00 P.M., Monday–Saturday; noon–5:00 P.M., Sunday
Credit Cards: American Express, Discover, MasterCard, Visa
Personal Checks: Yes, with proper identification
Handicapped Accessible: Yes
Bus Tours: Yes

Decker's
666 West Avenue

Directions: Exit 15 off I–95.
Phone: (203) 866–5593
Hours: 10:00 A.M.–6:00 P.M., Monday and Tuesday; 10:00 A.M.–8:00 P.M., Wednesday–Friday; 9:30 A.M.–5:30 P.M.; Saturday; noon–5:00 P.M., Sunday
Credit Cards: American Express, Discover, MasterCard, Visa
Personal Checks: Yes, with proper identification
Handicapped Accessible: Yes
Bus Tours: Yes

Dining In
541 Westport Avenue

Directions: Exit 16 off I–95; north on East Avenue to Route 1 (Westport Avenue).
Phone: (203) 846–4200
Hours: 9:30 A.M.–6:00 P.M., Monday–Wednesday; 9:30 A.M.–9:00 P.M, Thursday–Friday; 9:30 A.M.–6:00 P.M., Saturday; 11:00 A.M.–5:00 P.M., Sunday
Credit Cards: Discover, MasterCard, Visa
Personal Checks: Yes, with proper identification
Handicapped Accessible: No
Bus Tours: Yes

Factory Outlets at Norwalk
East Avenue

Directions: Take exit 16 off I–95; outlets are ⁹⁄₁₀ mile south.
Phone: (203) 838–1349
Hours: 10:00 A.M.–6:00 P.M., Monday–Wednesday and Saturday: 10:00 A.M.–9:00 P.M., Thursday–Friday; noon–5:00 P.M., Sunday
Bus Tours: Yes
Restaurants: D & D Eatery

Outlets:
Bag and Baggage
Bed, Bath, and Beyond
The Company Store
Famous Footwear
harvé benard
Just Coats and Swimwear
L'eggs/Hanes/Bali
Royal Doulton
Tanner
Van Heusen

Paper Warehouse
650 West Avenue

Directions: Exit 15 off I–95.
Phone: (203) 866–8492
Hours: 10:00 A.M.–5:30 P.M., Monday–Saturday; 11:00 A.M.–3:00 P.M.,
Sunday
Credit Cards: American Express, MasterCard, Visa
Personal Checks: Yes, with proper identification
Handicapped Accessible: Yes
Bus Tours: Yes

Pepperidge Farm
280 Connecticut Avenue

Directions: Call ahead.
Phone: (203) 838–9995
Hours: 9:00 A.M.–5:30 P.M., Monday–Friday; 9:00 A.M.–5:00 P.M., Saturday
Credit Cards: No
Personal Checks: Yes, Connecticut only, with proper identification
Handicapped Accessible: Yes
Bus Tours: Yes

Pro Golf Discount
437 Westport Avenue

Directions: Exit 16 off I–95 North or exit 17 off I–95 South to Route 1 (Westport Avenue). ·
Phone: (203) 846–4864
Hours: 10:00 A.M.–5:30 P.M., Monday-Thursday; 10:00 A.M.–8:00 P.M.; Friday; 10:00 A.M.–5:00 P.M., Saturday; 11:00 A.M.–4:00 P.M., Sunday except during January; hours change seasonally
Credit Cards: Discover, MasterCard, Visa,
Personal Checks: Yes, with proper identification
Handicapped Accessible: Yes
Bus Tours: No

Villeroy & Boch
Loehmann's Plaza
467 West Avenue

Directions: Exit 14 off I–95.
Phone: (203) 831–2821
Hours: 10:00 A.M.–6:00 P.M., Monday–Saturday; noon–6:00 P.M., Sunday
Credit Cards: MasterCard, Visa
Personal Checks: Yes, with proper identification
Handicapped Accessible: Yes
Bus Tours: Yes

Norwich

Arrow Paper Party Store
Great Plains Shopping Center
113 Salem Turnpike

Directions: Route 2 to Norwich to Chestnut Street.
Phone: (203) 889–5525
Hours: 9:00 A.M.–6:00 P.M., Monday–Saturday; 9:00 A.M.–8:00 P.M., Thursday; 10:00 A.M.–4:00 P.M., Sunday

Credit Cards: Discover, MasterCard, Visa
Personal Checks: Yes, with proper identification
Handicapped Accessible: No
Bus Tours: No

Gordon Shoe Outlet
35 Chestnut Street

Directions: Route 2 to Norwich to Chestnut Street.
Phone: (203) 889–9510
Hours: 9:00 A.M.–9:00 P.M., Monday–Friday; 9:00 A.M.–5:30 P.M., Saturday
Credit Cards: Discover, MasterCard, Visa
Personal Checks: Yes, with proper identification
Handicapped Accessible: No
Bus Tours: Yes

Old Lyme

Sudberry House
Colton Road

Directions: Exit 71 off I–95 to Four Mile River Road, left to Colton Road.
Phone: (203) 739–6951
Hours: 9:00 A.M.–4:30 P.M., Monday–Friday; 9:00 A.M.–1:00 P.M., Saturday, August and December only
Credit Cards: Discover, MasterCard, Visa
Personal Checks: Yes, with proper identification
Handicapped Accessible: Yes
Bus Tours: Yes

Orange

Black & Decker
481 Boston Post Road

Directions: Exit 39B off I–95 onto Route 1 (Boston Post Road).
Phone: (203) 795–3583
Hours: 9:00 A.M.–5:00 P.M., Monday–Friday; 9:00 A.M.–3:00 P.M., Saturday
Credit Cards: Discover, MasterCard, Visa
Personal Checks: Yes, with proper identification
Handicapped Accessible: Yes
Bus Tours: Yes

Pepperidge Farm
531 Boston Post Road

Directions: Call ahead.
Phone: (203) 795–6981
Hours: 9:00 A.M.–5:30 P.M., Monday–Friday; 9:00 A.M.–5:00 P.M., Saturday; noon–4:00 P.M., Sunday
Credit Cards: No
Personal Checks: Yes, United States, with proper identification
Handicapped Accessible: Yes
Bus Tours: Yes

Putnam

Wellington Curtain
Woodstock Avenue Plaza
Route 171

Directions: Exit 95 off Route 395 to Route 171.
Phone: (203) 928–7475
Hours: 10:00 A.M.–5:00 P.M., Monday–Friday; 10:00 A.M.–3:00 P.M., Saturday; closed Sunday
Credit Cards: American Express, Discover, MasterCard, Visa

Personal Checks: Yes, with proper identification
Handicapped Accessible: Yes
Bus Tours: Yes

Riverton

The Hitchcock Chair Store
Route 20

Directions: Route 44 West to Route 181 to Route 20.
Phone: (203) 379–4826
Hours: 10:00 A.M.–5:00 P.M., Monday–Wednesday and Saturday; 10:00 A.M.–6:00 P.M., Thursday; noon–5:00 P.M., Sunday
Credit Cards: Hitchcock, MasterCard, Visa
Personal Checks: Yes, with proper identification
Handicapped Accessible: Yes, partially
Bus Tours: Yes

Southport

Pepperidge Farm
3381 Post Road

Directions: Call ahead.
Phone: (203) 255–3671
Hours: 9:00 A.M.–6:00 P.M., Monday–Friday; 9:30 A.M.–5:00 P.M., Saturday; noon–4:00 P.M., Sunday
Credit Cards: No
Personal Checks: Yes, United States, with proper identification
Handicapped Accessible: No
Bus Tours: No

Stafford Springs

Warren of Stafford
29 Furnace Avenue

Directions: Route 32 to Furnace Avenue.
Phone: (203) 684–2766
Hours: 10:00 A.M.–5:00 P.M., Monday–Saturday
Credit Cards: MasterCard, Visa
Personal Checks: Yes, with proper identification
Handicapped Accessible: Yes
Bus Tours: Yes

Stamford

Hudson Paper Company
142 Hamilton Avenue

Directions: Exit 9 off I–95 to the Post Road to Portland Road to Hamilton Avenue.
Phone: (203) 324–1282
Hours: 9:00 A.M.–5:00 P.M., Monday–Saturday
Credit Cards: American Express, MasterCard, Visa
Personal Checks: Yes, with proper identification
Handicapped Accessible: No
Bus Tours: No

Stratford

Hudson Paper Company
1341 West Broad Street

Directions: Exit 32 off I–95 to West Broad Street.
Phone: (203) 378–0123
Hours: 9:00 A.M.–5:00 P.M., Monday–Saturday

Credit Cards: American Express, MasterCard, Visa
Personal Checks: Yes, with proper identification
Handicapped Accessible: Yes
Bus Tours: Yes

Wallingford

George S. Preisner Pewter
1177 North Colony Road, Route 5

Directions: Route 68 or Route 15 to Route 5.
Phone: (203) 265–0057
Hours: 10:30 A.M.–6:00 P.M., Monday–Saturday
Credit Cards: American Express, Discover, MasterCard, Visa
Personal Checks: Yes, with proper identification
Handicapped Accessible: Yes
Bus Tours: Yes

Waterbury

Distinctive Draperies
116 Homer Street

Directions: Exit 36 off Route 8 North.
Phone: (203) 574–2772; (800) 242–3727 (in Connecticut only)
Hours: 9:00 A.M.–5:00 P.M., Monday–Friday; 10:00 A.M.–4:00 P.M., Saturday
Credit Cards: No
Personal Checks: Yes, with proper identification
Handicapped Accessible: Yes
Bus Tours: Yes

Westport

Church's English Shoes
420 Post Road West (Route 1)

Directions: Exit 17 off I–95. Take Route 33 North for 2 miles to Route 1 West. Store is 1 mile on right.
Phone: (203) 454–4226
Hours: 10:00 A.M.–6:00 P.M., Monday–Saturday; noon–5:00 P.M., Sunday
Credit Cards: American Express, Diner's Card, MasterCard, Visa
Personal Checks: Yes, with proper identification
Handicapped Accessible: Yes
Bus Tours: Yes

Woodbury

Pepperidge Farm
Woodbury Shopping Square
107 Main Street North

Directions: Call ahead
Phone: (203) 263–5810
Hours: 9:30 A.M.–5:30 P.M., Monday–Friday; 9:30 A.M.–5:00 P.M., Saturday; 11:00 A.M.–4:00 P.M., Sunday
Credit Cards: No
Personal Checks: Yes, United States, with proper identification
Handicapped Accessible: Yes
Bus Tours: Yes

Can't remember what product a particular outlet offers? Check our "Profiles" section beginning on page one. Many listings also contain information on brand names and range of discounts.

Maine

Numbers at the left of this legend correspond to the numbers on the accompanying map. The number to the right of each city's or town's name is the page number on which that municipality's outlets first appear in this book.

1. Auburn, 75
2. Bangor, 75
3. Bar Harbor, 76
4. Brewer, 76
5. Brunswick, 77
6. Dexter, 77
7. Edgecomb, 77
8. Ellsworth, 78
9. Freeport, 79
10. Harmony, 82
11. Kittery, 83
12. Lewiston, 89
13. North Windham, 90

14. Oakland, 90
15. Oxford, 90
16. Presque Isle, 91
17. Rockport, 91
18. Saco, 92
19. Skowhegan, 92
20. South Portland, 93
21. Thomaston, 94
22. Waterville, 94
23. Wells, 95
24. Wilton, 96
25. Yarmouth, 96
26. York, 97

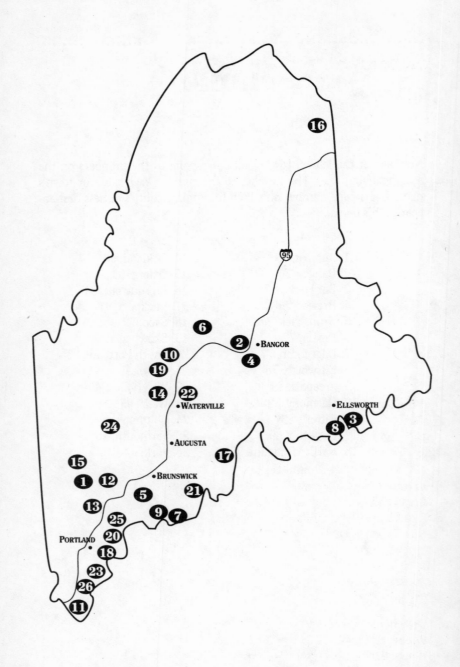

Auburn

Dexter Shoe
Route 4

Directions: Auburn exit of the Maine Turnpike to Route 4 North.
Phone: (207) 786–2292
Hours: 9:30 A.M.–8:00 P.M., Monday–Thursday; 9:30 A.M.–9:00 P.M., Friday; 9:00 A.M.–8:00 P.M., Saturday; 11:00 A.M.–5:00 P.M., Sunday
Credit Cards: MasterCard, Visa
Personal Checks: Yes, with proper identification
Handicapped Accessible: Yes
Bus tours: Yes

Bangor

Bass
Maine Square Mall
Hogan Road

Directions: I–95 North to exit 49; left at traffic light to Maine Square Mall.
Phone: (207) 942–8175
Hours: 9:00 A.M.–9:00 P.M., Monday–Saturday; 9:00 A.M.–5:00 P.M., Sunday; shorter winter hours
Credit Cards: American Express, Discover, MasterCard, Visa
Personal Checks: Yes, with proper identification
Handicapped Accessible: Yes
Bus Tours: Yes

Dexter Shoe
Hogan Road

Directions: Exit 49 off I–95 onto Hogan Road.
Phone: (207) 942–1776
Hours: 9:00 A.M.–9:00 P.M., Monday–Saturday; 10:00 A.M.–6:00 P.M., Sunday

Credit Cards: MasterCard, Visa
Personal Checks: Yes, with proper identification
Handicapped Accessible: Yes
Bus Tours: Yes

Bar Harbor

Timberland
44 Cottage Street

Directions: Call ahead.
Phone: (207) 288–9582
Hours: Open Memorial Day to Columbus Day 10:00 A.M.–6:00 P.M., Monday–Saturday and noon–5:00 P.M. Sunday; open July 4 to Labor Day 10:00 A.M.–10:00 P.M., Monday–Saturday
Credits Cards: American Express, Discover, MasterCard, Visa
Personal Checks: Yes, with proper identification

Brewer

Dexter Shoe
Wilson Street

Directions: Route 1A (Wilson Street) from Bangor across Chamberlain Bridge.
Phone: (207) 989–3185
Hours: 9:00 A.M.–8:00 P.M., Monday–Saturday; 10:00 A.M.–5:00 P.M., Sunday; shorter winter hours
Credit Cards: MasterCard, Visa
Personal Checks: Yes, with proper identification
Handicapped Accessible: Yes
Bus Tours: Yes

Brunswick

Dexter Shoe
Outer Pleasant Street

Directions: I–95 to Route 1 exit, Brunswick (Outer Pleasant Street).
Phone: (207) 729–0002
Hours: 9:00 A.M.–9:00 P.M., Monday–Saturday; 10:00 A.M.–7:00 P.M., Sunday; shorter winter hours
Credit Cards: MasterCard, Visa
Personal Checks: Yes, with proper identification
Handicapped Accessible: Yes
Bus Tours: Yes

Dexter

Dexter Shoe
Church Street (Route 7)

Directions: Newport exit and Route 7 off I–95 toward Moosehead Lake region and the Dexter plant.
Phone: (207) 924–3237
Hours: 9:00 A.M.–6:00 P.M., Monday-Saturday; 10:00 A.M.–5:00 P.M. Sunday
Credit Cards: MasterCard, Visa
Personal Checks: Yes, with proper identification
Handicapped Accessible: Yes
Bus Tours: Yes

Edgecomb

Dexter Shoe
Route 1

Directions: Route 1, north of the Wiscasset Bridge.
Phone: (207) 882–6735

Hours: 9:00 A.M.–8:00 P.M., Monday–Saturday; 10:00 A.M.–6:00 P.M., Sunday; shorter winter hours
Credit Cards: MasterCard, Visa
Personal Checks: Yes, with proper identification
Handicapped Accessible: Yes
Bus Tours: Yes

Ellsworth

Bass
Maine Coast Mall
Routes 1 and 3

Directions: Route 2 into Ellsworth to the junction of routes 1 and 3 at Maine Coast Mall.
Phone: (207) 667–5012
Hours: 9:00 A.M.–9:00 P.M., Monday–Saturday; 9:00 A.M.–6:00 P.M., Sunday; shorter winter hours
Credit Cards: MasterCard, Visa
Personal Checks: Yes, with proper identification
Handicapped Accessible: Yes
Bus Tours: Yes

Dexter Shoe
Bar Harbor Road

Directions: Route 3 is Bar Harbor Road.
Phone: (207) 667–8831
Hours: 9:00 A.M.–9:00 P.M., Monday–Saturday; 10:00 A.M.–7:00 P.M., Sunday; shorter winter hours
Credit Cards: MasterCard, Visa
Personal Checks: Yes, with proper identification
Handicapped Accessible: Yes
Bus Tours: Yes

Ellsworth Outlet Center
150 High Street

Directions: Junction of Route 1 and Route 3.
Phone: (207) 667-7753
Hours: 9:00 A.M.–6:00 P.M., Sunday–Thursday; 9:00 A.M.–8:00 P.M., Friday–
Saturday
Handicapped Accessible: Yes
Bus Tours: Yes
Outlets:
Corning/Revere
L. L. Bean
London Fog

*Freeport

Freeport is not only the home of L. L. Bean (open 24 hours a day, 365
days a year); it is also one of the "outlet capitals" of New England.
Freeport accommodates outlet shoppers with large parking lots, des-
ignated lots for buses on tour, and special loading zones in town for
bus tours. Be sure to stop at one of the visitors' kiosks on Main Street
for a walking map.

Directions: I–95 to exit 19 to Route 1 east.
Phone: For information on individual stores, call the Freeport Mer-
chants Association at (207) 865–1212. They have a complete listing of
stores.
Hours: Summer hours (Memorial Day through Labor Day) are typically
10:00 A.M.–9:00 P.M., Monday–Saturday and 10:00 A.M.–6:00 P.M., Sunday;
some outlets open earlier. The rest of the year hours are typically 10:00
A.M.–6:00 P.M., Monday–Sunday, with some outlets staying open later on
Friday and Saturday. Call ahead to confirm hours of operation if you
will be shopping at an "off time," particularly if there is a special outlet
you wish to visit.
Bus Tours: Yes

Dexter Village
Route 1

Directions: I–95 to exit 19 to Route 1 east.
Phone: (207) 865–6626 (Dexter)
Hours: See Freeport, above
Outlets:
Dexter Shoe
Levi's

Fashion Outlet Mall
2 Depot Street, downtown Freeport area

Directions: I–95 to exit 19 to Route 1 east.
Phone: See Freeport, page 79
Hours: See Freeport, page 79
Restaurants: A variety on and off Main Street from which to choose
Outlets:
Anne Klein
Bag and Baggage
Bogner
Cannon
Fila
Maidenform
Polly Flinders

Freeport Crossing
200 Lower Main Street, Route 1

Directions: I–95 to exit 19 to Route 1 east.
Phone: See Freeport, page 79
Hours: See Freeport, page 79
Restaurants: A variety on and off Main Street from which to choose
Outlets:
Bass
Carter's
NordicTrack

Reebok/Rockport
Van Heusen

Freeport Downtown Main Street Area

Note: Although downtown Freeport is not an outlet mall, the stores are numerous and located near one another and, thus, are grouped together here.

Main Street, Bow Street, West Street, etc.

Directions: I–95 to exit 19 to Route 1 east.
Phone: See Freeport, page 79
Hours: See Freeport, page 79
Bus Tours: Yes
Restaurants: A variety on and off Main Street from which to choose
Outlets:
Alpine Sheets and Towels
American Tourister
Arrow
Banana Republic
Banister Shoe
Barbizon
Bass
Bed & Bath
Benetton
Bogner
Boston Traders
Brooks Brothers
Bugle Boy
Buttons and Things
Calvin Klein
Cambridge Dry Goods
Coach
Cole-Haan Shoes
Corning/Revere
Crabtree and Evelyn
Cuddletown
Dansk

Donna Karan
Dooney & Bourke
Eagle's Eye
Fanny Farmer
Fila
Hathaway/Warners/Olga
Izod/Gant
J. Crew
Johnston & Murphy Shoes
Jones New York
Laura Ashley
L'eggs/Hanes/Bali
L. L. Bean Outlet
London Fog
Maine Wreath and Flower
Mikasa
nautica
Patagonia
Pepperidge Farm
Polo/Ralph Lauren
Ribbon Outlet
Timberland
totes
Villeroy & Boch
Yankee Candle

Harmony

Bartlett Yarns
20 Water Street

Directions: Exit 36 off Maine Turnpike to Route 201 to Skowhegan to
Route 150 to Water Street in Harmony.
Phone: (207) 683–2251
Hours: 8:30 A.M.–4:00 P.M., Monday–Friday
Credit Cards: No

Personal Checks: Yes, with proper identification
Handicapped Accessible: Yes
Bus Tours: Yes

*Kittery

Kittery is an outlet shopper's paradise. Many new outlet centers have sprung up along both sides of Route 1 in the past few years. Kittery now rivals Freeport as an "outlet capital" of New England.

Directions: I–95 to exit 3 to Coastal Route 1.
Phone: For information on individual stores, call the Kittery/Eliot Chamber of Commerce at (800) 639–9645. They have a complete listing of stores.
Hours: 10:00 A.M.–6:00 P.M., Monday–Saturday; noon–6:00 P.M., Sunday. Some outlets open earlier and some stay open until 9:00 P.M., especially on Friday and Saturday. Call ahead to confirm hours if you will be shopping at an "off time," particularly if there is a special outlet you want to visit.
Handicapped Accessible: Most, but not all, outlets
Restaurants: A variety from which to choose, including McDonald's and Burger King
Attractions: Kittery Trading Post, although not an outlet, is a must for any outdoor enthusiast. It's chock-full of fishing, hunting, camping, canoeing, and archery gear, as well as clothing for the outdoor life.

Dansk Square Outlets
Route 1

Phone: See Kittery, above
Hours: See Kittery, above
Outlets:
Dansk
Fieldcrest/Cannon
Top of the Line Cosmetics and Fragrances

Dexter Shoe
Route 1

Phone: (207) 439–3667
Hours: See Kittery, page 83
Credit Cards: MasterCard, Visa
Personal Checks: Yes, with proper identification
Handicapped Accessible: Yes
Bus Tours: Yes

Kittery Outlet Center
Route 1

Phone: See Kittery, page 83
Hours: See Kittery, page 83
Outlets:
Book Warehouse
Cape Isle Knitters
Le Sportsac
Levi's
Royal Doulton
Stride Rite/Keds/Sperry Top-Sider
totes
Van Heusen
Waterford/Wedgwood
Westport, Ltd.

Kittery Outlet Village
Route 1

Phone: See Kittery, page 83
Hours: See Kittery, page 83
Outlets:
Bagmakers
Crate and Barrel
Etienne Aigner
J. Crew

Jones New York
Napier Jewelry
Polo/Ralph Lauren

Kittery Place
Route 1

Phone: See Kittery, page 83
Hours: See Kittery, page 83
Outlets:
Esprit
Fitz and Floyd
Izod/Gant
nautica
Socks Galore and More
Sunglass Outlet

Maine Gate Outlet
Route 1

Phone: See Kittery, page 83
Hours: See Kittery, page 83
Outlets:
Corning/Revere
Eddie Bauer
Kitchen Collection/Proctor Silex/Wearever
Leather Loft
9 West

The Maine Outlet
Route 1

Phone: See Kittery, page 83
Hours: See Kittery, page 83
Handicapped Accessible: Yes
Restaurants: Noel's Restaurant & Bakery

Outlets:
Arrow
Bag and Baggage
Banister Shoe
Book and Music Outlet
Champion/Hanes
The Children's Outlet
Donna Karan
Famous Brands Housewares
Fuller Brush
Gund
Hathaway/Warners/Olga
HE-RO Group
J. H. Collectibles
Leather Loft
L'eggs/Hanes/Bali
Linens 'n Things
Mikasa
Naturalizer
Oneida Silver
Samuel Robert
Timberland

Manufacturer's Outlet Mall
318 Route 1

Phone: See Kittery, page 83
Hours: See Kittery, page 83
Outlets:
Bose
Chuck Roast
FAO Schwarz
harvé benard
Villeroy & Boch
Yankee Candle

Outlet Mall of Kittery
Route 1

Phone: See Kittery, page 83
Hours: See Kittery, page 83
Outlets:
Casual Male
Guess? Again
Ribbon Outlet
Sox Market

Pepperidge Farm
Route 1

Directions: Call ahead.
Phone: (207) 439–6051
Hours: See Kittery, page 83
Credit Cards: No
Personal Checks: Yes, with proper identification

Spruce Creek Outlet Mall
Route 1

Phone: See Kittery, page 83
Hours: See Kittery, page 83
Outlets:
Bugle Boy
Converse
Famous Footwear
London Fog
Prestige Fragrance and Cosmetics

Tanger Outlet Center I
Route 1

Phone: See Kittery, page 83
Hours: 10:00 A.M.–9:00 P.M., Monday–Saturday; 10:00 A.M.–6:00 P.M., Sunday
Outlets:
American Tourister
Anne Klein
Bass
Black & Decker
Carter's
Geoffrey Beene
L'eggs/Hanes/Bali
Liz Claiborne
OshKosh B'Gosh
Van Heusen
Wallet Works

Tanger Factory Outlet Center II
Route 1

Phone: (800) 727–6885
Hours: See Kittery, page 83
Handicapped Accessible: Yes
Outlets:
Adrienne Vittadini
Brooks Brothers
Calvin Klein
Eagle's Eye
Maidenform
Samsonite

Tidewater Mall
375 Route 1

Phone: See Kittery, page 83
Hours: See Kittery, page 83
Outlets:
Boston Traders
Chaus
Genuine Kids
Hickey-Freeman
Jewelry Mine
Lenox China
Magnavox
North Country Leathers
Pfaltzgraff
Reed & Barton Silversmiths

Lewiston

Bates Mill Store
Bates Complex Building
Chestnut Street

Directions: Exit 13 off I–95, north on Lisbon Street. Left at traffic light onto Chestnut Street.
Phone: (207) 784–7626
Hours: 9:00 A.M.–4:00 P.M., Monday–Friday; 9:00 A.M.–1:00 P.M., Saturday
Credit Cards: MasterCard, Visa
Personal Checks: Yes, with proper identification
Handicapped Accessible: Yes
Bus Tours: Yes

North Windham

Dexter Shoe
Route 302

Directions: Exit 8 off the Maine Turnpike; follow Route 302 to North Windham.
Phone: (207) 892–2424
Hours: 9:00 A.M.–8:00 P.M., Monday–Saturday; 10:00 A.M.–5:00 P.M., Sunday; shorter winter hours
Credit Cards: MasterCard, Visa
Personal Checks: Yes, with proper identification
Handicapped Accessible: Yes
Bus Tours: Yes

Oakland

Cascade Woolen Mill
Route 137 at Route 23

Directions: Waterville–Oakland exit off I–95 to Route 137.
Phone: (207) 465–9080
Hours: 10:00 A.M.–5:00 P.M., Monday–Saturday
Credit Cards: MasterCard, Visa
Personal Checks: Yes, with proper identification
Handicapped Accessible: Yes
Bus Tours: Yes

Oxford

Oxford Mill End Store
King Street

Directions: Exit 11 off Maine Turnpike at Gray to Route 26 to Route 121.

Phone: (207) 539–4451
Hours: 9:00 A.M.–5:00 P.M., Monday–Saturday
Credit Cards: No
Personal Checks: Yes, with proper identification
Handicapped Accessible: Yes
Bus Tours: Yes

Presque Isle

Dexter Shoe
Route 1

Directions: Route 1, north of business district.
Phone: (207) 764–0708
Hours: 9:30 A.M.–5:00 P.M., Monday–Thursday; 9:30 A.M.–8:00 P.M., Friday; 9:00 A.M.–6:00 P.M., Saturday
Credit Cards: MasterCard, Visa
Personal Checks: Yes, with proper identification
Handicapped Accessible: Yes
Bus Tours: Yes

Rockport

Dexter Shoe
Route 1 (Commercial Street)

Directions: Follow Route 1 (Commercial Street) to the Glen Cove area of Rockport.
Phone: (207) 594–2001
Hours: 9:00 A.M.–8:00 P.M., Monday–Saturday; 10:00 A.M.–6:00 P.M., Sunday; shorter winter hours
Credit Cards: MasterCard, Visa
Personal Checks: Yes, with proper identification
Handicapped Accessible: Yes
Bus Tours: Yes

Saco

Dexter Shoe
Route 1

Directions: Maine Turnpike to exit 5, Route 1 North.
Phone: (207) 282–1694
Hours: 9:00 A.M.–9:00 P.M., Monday–Saturday; 10:00 A.M.–7:00 P.M., Sunday; shorter winter hours
Credit Cards: MasterCard, Visa
Personal Checks: Yes, with proper identification
Handicapped Accessible: Yes, partially
Bus Tours: Yes

Skowhegan

Dexter Shoe
Route 2, West Front Street

Directions: I–95 north to the Skowhegan exit to Route 201 North.
Phone: (207) 474–5530
Hours: 9:00 A.M.–6:00 P.M., Monday–Thursday; 9:00 A.M.–8:00 P.M., Friday; 9:00 A.M.–6:00 P.M., Saturday; 10:00 A.M.–5:00 P.M., Sunday; shorter winter hours
Credit Cards: MasterCard, Visa
Personal Checks: Yes, with proper identification
Handicapped Accessible: Yes
Bus Tours: Yes

New Balance
13 Walnut Street

Directions: I–95 to exit 36. Follow Route 201 North approximately 14½ miles. Turn in next to bank at corner of Route 201 and Walnut Street.
Phone: (207) 474–6231
Hours: 9:00 A.M.–5:00 P.M., Monday–Thursday and Saturday; 9:00

A.M.–7:00 P.M., Friday; noon–5:00 P.M., Sundays May–December only
Credit Cards: American Express, MasterCard, Visa
Personal Checks: Yes, with proper identification
Handicapped Accessible: Yes, on first floor

South Portland

Bass
335 Maine Mall Road

Directions: I–95 to Maine Mall Road and continue to the store opposite the mall.
Phone: (207) 772–2829
Hours: 9:00 A.M.–9:00 P.M., Monday–Saturday; 10:00 A.M.–6:00 P.M., Sunday
Credit Cards: American Express, Discover, MasterCard, Visa
Personal Checks: Yes, with proper identification
Handicapped Accessible: Yes
Restaurants: Friendly's
Bus Tours: Yes

Dexter Shoe
Westbrook Street

Directions: From I–295 North, take the Route 1–South Portland exit, then the Broadway–South Portland exit. From I–295 South, take the Westbrook Street–Airport exit.
Phone: (207) 774–7917
Hours: 9:30 A.M.–9:00 P.M., Monday–Saturday; 11:00 A.M.–6:00 P.M., Sunday; extended seasonal hours
Credit Cards: MasterCard, Visa
Personal Checks: Yes, with proper identification
Handicapped Accessible: Yes
Bus Tours: Yes

Thomaston

Barnes Window Treatment
Route 1

Directions: Coastal Route 1 to Thomaston.
Phone: (207) 354–6830
Hours: 9:00 A.M.–5:00 P.M., Monday–Friday; 10:00 A.M.–4:00 P.M., Saturday
Credit Cards: MasterCard, Visa
Personal Checks: Yes, with proper identification
Handicapped Accessible: No
Bus Tours: Yes

Maine State Prison Showroom
Route 1

Directions: Take Route 1 to Thomaston; the shop is right on Route 1.
Phone: (207) 354–2535
Hours: 9:00 A.M.–5:00 P.M. every day
Credit Cards: MasterCard, Visa
Personal Checks: Yes, with proper identification
Handicapped Accessible: No
Bus Tours: Yes

Waterville

Dexter Shoe
Kennedy Memorial Drive

Directions: Take the Waterville–Oakland exit from I–95 to Waterville.
Phone: (207) 873–5858
Hours: 9:00 A.M.–9:00 P.M., Monday–Saturday; 10:00 A.M.–6:00 P.M., Sunday; shorter winter hours
Credit Cards: MasterCard, Visa
Personal Checks: Yes, with proper identification
Handicapped Accessible: Yes, partially
Bus Tours: Yes

Wells

Bass
Wells Plaza
Route 1

Directions: Exit 2 off Interstate 95, take a left after toll booths, come to light on Wells Corner, take a right. Bass is across from McDonald's in the Shop-n-Save Plaza.
Phone: (207) 646–5237
Hours: 9:00 A.M.–9:00 P.M., Monday–Saturday; 10:00 A.M.–5:00 P.M., Sunday
Credit Cards: American Express, Discover, MasterCard, Visa
Personal Checks: Yes, with proper identification
Handicapped Accessible: Yes
Bus Tours: Yes

Dexter Shoe
Route 1

Directions: Maine Turnpike exit 2 to Route 109 Wells. The store is on Route 1.
Phone: (207) 646–7557
Hours: Summer, 9:00 A.M.–9:00 P.M., Monday–Saturday, and 10:00 A.M.–8:00 P.M., Sunday; winter, 9:30 A.M.–5:00 P.M., Monday–Saturday, and 10:00 A.M.–5:00 P.M., Sunday
Credit Cards: MasterCard, Visa
Personal Checks: Yes, with proper identification
Handicapped Accessible: Yes, partially
Bus Tours: Yes

Remember that outlets accepting personal checks usually require at least two forms of proper identification, usually a driver's license and a major credit card.

Wilton

Bass
Routes 2 and 4

Directions: Route 4 North from Auburn to Wilton. The store is at the intersection of Routes 2 and 4.
Phone: (207) 645–2072
Hours: 9:00 A.M.–9:00 P.M., Monday–Saturday; 10:00 A.M.–6:00 P.M., Sunday; shorter winter hours
Credit Cards: Discover, MasterCard, Visa
Personal Checks: Yes, with proper identification
Handicapped Accessible: No
Bus Tours: Yes

Dexter Shoe
Route 2

Directions: Route 2, 1 mile east of the junction with Route 156.
Phone: (207) 645–4200
Hours: 9:30 A.M.–6:00 P.M., Monday–Saturday; 10:00 A.M.–5:00 P.M., Sunday
Credit Cards: MasterCard, Visa
Personal Checks: Yes, with proper identification
Handicapped Accessible: Yes
Bus Tours: Yes

Yarmouth

Howard's
Route 1

Directions: Exit 16 or exit 17 off I–295 to Route 1. Follow Coastal Route 1 to the store.
Phone: (207) 846–5912
Hours: 9:30 A.M.–5:30 P.M., Monday–Saturday; 11:00 A.M.–5:00 P.M.; Sunday

Credit Cards: American Express, Discover, MasterCard, Visa
Personal Checks: Yes, with proper identification
Handicapped Accessible: Yes
Bus Tours: Yes

York

Dexter Shoe
Route 1

Directions: From I–95 take the exit at York and go north on Route 1.
Phone: (207) 363–6664
Hours: 9:30 A.M.–8:00 P.M., Monday–Saturday; 10:00 A.M.–6:00 P.M., Sunday; shorter winter hours
Credit Cards: MasterCard, Visa
Personal Checks: Yes, with proper identification
Handicapped Accessible: Yes
Bus Tours: Yes

Can't remember what product a particular outlet offers? Check our "Profiles" section beginning on page one. Many listings also contain information on brand names and range of discounts.

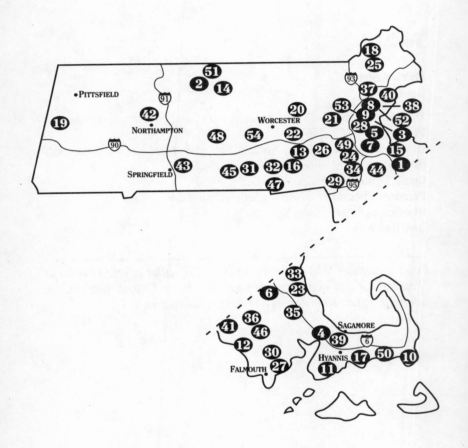

Massachusetts

Numbers at the left of this legend correspond to the numbers on the accompanying map. The number to the right of each city's or town's name is the page number on which that municipality's outlets first appear in this book.

1. Avon, 100
2. Baldwinville, 100
3. Boston, 101
4. Bourne, 101
5. Brighton, 102
6. Brockton, 102
7. Brookline, 103
8. Burlington, 103
9. Cambridge, 104
10. Chatham, 104
11. East Falmouth, 105
12. Fall River, 105
13. Framingham, 109
14. Gardner, 110
15. Hingham, 111
16. Holliston, 112
17. Hyannis, 112
18. Lawrence, 113
19. Lenox, 114
20. Littleton, 114
21. Malden, 115
22. Marlborough, 115
23. Marshfield, 116
24. Medfield, 116
25. Middleton, 116
26. Natick, 117
27. New Bedford, 117

28. Newton, 119
29. North Attleboro, 119
30. North Dartmouth, 119
31. North Oxford, 121
32. Northbridge, 121
33. Norwell, 121
34. Norwood, 122
35. Pembroke, 123
36. Raynham, 123
37. Reading, 124
38. Revere, 124
39. Sagamore, 125
40. Saugus, 126
41. Seekonk, 126
42. South Deerfield, 127
43. Springfield, 127
44. Stoughton, 128
45. Sturbridge, 128
46. Taunton, 129
47. Uxbridge, 130
48. Ware, 130
49. Westwood, 131
50. West Yarmouth, 131
51. Winchendon, 132
52. Winthrop, 132
53. Woburn, 133
54. Worcester, 133

Avon

Forecaster of Boston
Avon Industrial Park
Strafellow Drive

Directions: Take exit 19A off Route 24. At traffic light past end of ramp, take left into Avon Industrial Park. Take Strafellow Drive to end. Forecaster is on right.
Phone: (508) 586–1848
Hours: 9:30 A.M.–4:30 P.M., Monday–Saturday
Credit Cards: Discover, MasterCard, Visa
Personal Checks: Yes, with proper identification
Handicapped Accessible: Yes
Bus Tours: Yes

Baldwinville

Dan's Pine Shop
46 Elm Street

Directions: Route 2 West to Baldwinville Road exit, right to Route 202 North.
Phone: (508) 939–5687
Hours: 10:00 A.M.–5:00 P.M., Monday–Saturday; 1:00–5:00 P.M., Sunday
Credit Cards: Discover, MasterCard, Visa
Personal Checks: Yes, with proper identification
Handicapped Accessible: No
Bus Tours: Yes

Boston

Eddie Bauer
Devonshire Place
230 Washington Street

Directions: On the Freedom Trail, in the heart of Boston. Take the T to Downtown Crossing stop.
Phone: (617) 227–4840
Hours: 10:00 A.M.–6:00 P.M., Monday–Saturday; noon–5:00 P.M. Sunday
Credit Cards: American Express, MasterCard, Visa, Eddie Bauer FCNB charge, Spiegel Card
Personal Checks: Yes, with proper identification
Handicapped Accessible: Yes
Bus Tours: No

Bourne

Tanger Outlet Center
Route 28

Directions: Route 28 at the Bourne rotary.
Phone: (800) 727–6885
Hours: 10:00 A.M.–6:00 P.M., Monday–Wednesday and Friday–Saturday; 10:00 A.M.–7:00 P.M., Thursday; noon–6:00 P.M. Sunday, some outlets open until 9:00 P.M. weekdays during the summer
Handicapped Accessible: Yes
Outlets:
Adolfo II
Barbizon Lingerie
Cape Isle Knitters
Levi's
Liz Claiborne

Brighton

New Balance
61 North Beacon Street

Directions: I–90 to the Alston/Cambridge exit. Turn left onto Cambridge Street. At fifth light, turn right onto Beacon Street.
Phone: (617) 782–0803
Hours: 9:30 A.M.–7 P.M., Monday–Saturday; noon–6:00 P.M., Sunday
Credit Cards: American Express, MasterCard, Visa
Personal Checks: Yes, with proper identification
Handicapped Accessible: Yes
Bus Tours: No

Brockton

Knapp Shoe
1285 Belmont Street

Directions: Route 24 to exit 17.
Phone: (508) 588–9009
Hours: 9:30 A.M.–6:00 P.M., Monday–Saturday; noon–5:00 P.M., Sunday
Credit Cards: Discover, MasterCard, Visa
Personal Checks: Yes, with proper identification
Handicapped Accessible: Yes
Bus Tours: Yes

Mackintosh New England
Shaw's Plaza
607 Belmont Street

Directions: From Route 24, take exit 17A to Route 123 to Belmont Street. Follow to Shaw's Plaza.
Phone: (508) 559–0847

Hours: 10:00 A.M.–6:00 P.M., Monday–Wednesday and Saturday; 10:00 A.M.–8:00 P.M., Thursday–Friday; noon–5:00 P.M., Sunday
Credit Cards: MasterCard, Visa
Personal Checks: Yes, with proper identification

Brookline

China Fair Warehouse
1638 Beacon Street

Directions: From Boston take Beacon Street into Brookline.
Phone: (617) 566–2220
Hours: 9:30 A.M.–5:15 P.M., Monday–Saturday
Credit Cards: No
Personal Checks: Yes, Massachusetts, with proper identification
Handicapped Accessible: No
Bus Tours: No

Burlington

Pepperidge Farm
Middlesex Mall
43 Middlesex Turnpike

Directions: Call ahead.
Phone: (617) 272–5158
Hours: 10:00 A.M.–9:00 P.M., Monday–Friday; 10:00 A.M.–6:00 P.M., Saturday; noon–5:00 P.M. Sunday
Credit Cards: No
Personal Checks: Yes, United States, with proper identification
Handicapped Accessible: Yes
Bus Tours: No

Cambridge

China Fair Warehouse
2100 Massachusetts Avenue

Directions: Massachusetts Avenue is a main thoroughfare through Cambridge and is easy to find.
Phone: (617) 864–3050
Hours: 10:00 A.M.–6:00 P.M., Monday–Saturday; 10:00 A.M.–5:00 P.M., Sunday during Christmas season
Credit Cards: No
Personal Checks: Yes, Massachusetts, with proper identification
Handicapped Accessible: Yes
Restaurants: McDonald's

Pepperidge Farm
87 Blanchard Road

Directions: Call ahead.
Phone: (617) 661–6361
Hours: 9:00 A.M.–6:00 P.M., Monday–Friday; 9:00 A.M.–5:00 P.M., Saturday; noon–4:00 P.M., Sunday
Credit Cards: No
Personal Checks: Yes, United States, with proper identification
Handicapped Accessible: Yes
Bus Tours: No

Chatham

Van Heusen
1238 Main Street

Directions: Call ahead.
Phone: (508) 945–4063 or 945–4062
Hours: 9:00 A.M.–9:00 P.M., Monday–Saturday; noon–5:00 P.M., Sunday
Credit Cards: American Express, Discover, MasterCard, Visa

Personal Checks: Yes, with proper identification
Handicapped Accessible: Yes
Bus Tours: No

East Falmouth

Kenyon's Corners
767–79 Main Street

Directions: Route 28 to Central Avenue.
Phone: No central phone number
Hours: 10:00 A.M.–6:00 P.M., Monday–Saturday; noon–6:00 P.M., Sunday; some outlets stay open until 9:00 P.M. during the summer
Outlets:
Aileen
L'eggs/Hanes/Bali

*Fall River

The city of Fall River is one of the more extensive factory outlet areas in New England. You can shop all day; clothing, curtains, giftware, and innumerable other items are available at excellent savings. Many of the stores are clustered together in the old mills and are easily spotted because of their red heart identification marks.

Near Fall River is the city of New Bedford, with more factory outlet opportunities.

Directions:
From Boston: Take Route 24 South to exit 41 West, follow 195 a short distance, then take exit 8A to Route 24 South and exit 2, Brayton Avenue. Take a left onto Brayton Avenue and first right onto Jefferson Street.
From Hartford: Take Route 2 East to Route 11 South to Route 85 South, then I–95 North to Providence. Take 195 East to exit 8A (Route

24 South), then exit 2, Brayton Avenue. Take a left onto Brayton Avenue and first right onto Jefferson Street.

From New Bedford and Cape Cod: Take 195 West to exit 8A (Route 24 South), then exit 2, Brayton Avenue. Take a left onto Brayton Avenue and first right onto Jefferson Street.

From Newport: Take Route 24 North to exit 2, Brayton Avenue. Take a left onto Brayton Avenue and first right onto Jefferson Street.

From Providence: Take 195 East to exit 8A (Route 24 South), then exit 2, Brayton Avenue. Take a left onto Brayton Avenue and first right onto Jefferson Street.

Bag Outlet
Plymouth Avenue

Directions: Call ahead.
Phone: (508) 674–0530
Hours: 9:00 A.M.–5:00 P.M., Monday–Saturday
Credit Cards: MasterCard, Visa
Personal Checks: Yes, with proper identification
Handicapped Accessible: Yes
Restaurants: Burger King
Bus Tours: Yes

Cotton Mill
109 Howe Street

Directions: Off Route 138 South.
Phone: (508) 674–9499 or (800) 370–6455
Hours: 9:30 A.M.–5:00 P.M., Tuesday–Friday; open noon–5:00 P.M., Sunday and Monday September 15 to December 15 and March 15 to June 15
Credit Cards: Discover, MasterCard, Visa
Handicapped Accessible: Yes
Bus Tours: Yes

Wampanoag Mill Factory Outlet Center
420 Quequechan Street

Directions: Call ahead.
Phone: (508) 678–5242
Hours: 9:00 A.M.–5:00 P.M., Monday–Saturday; noon–5:00 P.M., Sunday; some outlets open Friday evenings; extended holiday hours
Handicapped Accessible: Yes
Restaurants: Fall River Cafe
Bus Tours: Yes
Outlets:
Curtain Factory Outlet
Parker's Candies

Louis Hand
847 Pleasant Street

Directions: I–195 East to exit 7 onto Plymouth Avenue; left, then right at second set of lights onto Pleasant Street.
Phone: (508) 674–2326
Hours: 9:00 A.M.–5:00 P.M., Monday–Wednesday and Saturday; 9:00 A.M.–8:30 P.M., Thursday–Friday
Credit Cards: Discover, MasterCard, Visa
Personal Checks: Yes, with proper identification
Bus Tours: Yes

Quality Factory Outlets
638 Quequechan Street, in the Shawmut Mill

Directions: Call ahead.
Phone: (508) 677–4949
Hours: 9:00 A.M.–6:00 P.M., Monday–Saturday; noon–6:00 P.M., Sunday; most outlets open Friday evenings; extended holiday hours
Handicapped Accessible: Yes
Restaurants: Ana's Cafe and Restaurant
Bus Tours: Yes

Outlets:
Aileen
Bass
Bugle Boy
Carter's
Corning/Revere
Factory Party Outlet
Famous Footwear
Farberware
Levi's
Libbey Glass
London Fog
Manhattan
Micki Designer Separates
Ribbon Outlet
Saucony Soft-Bilt Athletic Shoes
Swank
Van Heusen

Sandpiper Creations
1 West Street

Directions: I–195 to Fall River; at Braga Bridge take Route 79 North to North Main Street exit. Take a right onto North Main Street, then take first right (Weaver Street). Take a left at the end of Weaver Street onto West Street.
Phone: (508) 678–3202
Hours: 9:00 A.M.–5:00 P.M., Monday–Friday; 9:00 A.M.–4:00 P.M., Saturday; noon–4:00 P.M., Sunday in summer only
Credit Cards: MasterCard, Visa
Personal Checks: Yes, with proper identification
Handicapped Accessible: No
Bus Tours: Yes

Tower Outlet Center
657 Quarry Street, in the Barnard Mills

Directions: Call ahead.
Phone: (508) 678–6033
Hours: 9:00 A.M.–5:00 P.M., Monday–Saturday; noon–5:00 P.M., Sunday; some outlets open Friday evenings; extended holiday hours
Handicapped Accessible: Yes
Restaurants: Auntie Anna's Eatery
Bus Tours: Yes
Outlets:
Izod/Gant
Leather Loft
L'eggs/Hanes/Bali
Stetson Hat

Trina
Ace Street

Directions: Call ahead.
Phone: (508) 678–7605
Hours: 9:00 A.M.–4:00 P.M., Monday–Friday; 9:00 A.M.–2:00 P.M., Saturday
Feature: This outlet is located at the factory.
Credit Cards: MasterCard, Visa
Personal Checks: Yes, with proper identification
Handicapped Acessible: No
Bus Tours: Yes

Framingham

Frugal Fannie's
New York Avenue

Directions: From Route 9 West, take first right after Sheraton Tara onto California Avenue. Take first left onto New York Avenue to last building on the far right. Look for yellow awnings.

Phone: (508) 872–5800
Hours: Typically 8:00 A.M.–6:00 P.M., Saturday and noon–5:00 P.M., Sunday. Closed for vacation from around July 4 to before Labor Day. Always call ahead; a recorded message gives current hours.
Additional Savings: Clean Sweep, twice a year; annual coat, suit, separates sales. Mailing list.
Credit Cards: Discover, MasterCard, Visa
Personal Checks: Yes, with proper identification
Handicapped Accessible: No

Gardner

Gardner Furniture
25 Craft Street

Directions: Take Route 2 to exit 22. Take Route 68 South. Turn left at light onto Route 2A East, which is East Broadway. Store is at corner of East Broadway and Craft.
Phone: (508) 632–9661 or (508) 632–1930 or (800) 244–9661
Hours: 8:00 A.M.–5:00 P.M., Monday–Wednesday and Saturday; 8:00 A.M.–8:00 P.M., Thursday–Friday; noon–5:00 P.M., Sunday
Credit Cards: MasterCard, Visa
Personal Checks: Yes, with proper identification

Nothing But 2nds
45 Logan Street

Directions: Located in the basement level of The Factory Coop. Take Route 2 to exit 23. Bear right at bottom of ramp, under railroad bridge. Go straight through lights, then take second left.
Phone: (508) 632–1447
Hours: 9:00 A.M.–5:00 P.M., Monday–Friday; 9:00 A.M.–6:00 P.M., Saturday; noon–5:00 P.M., Sunday
Credit Cards: MasterCard, Visa
Personal Checks: Yes, with proper identification

R. Smith Furniture
289 South Main Street

Directions: Exit 23 off Route 2.
Phone: (508) 632–3461 or 632–3477
Hours: 8:00 A.M.–5:00 P.M., Monday–Thursday and Saturday; 8:00 A.M.–9:00 P.M., Friday; 1:00–5:00 P.M., Sunday
Credit Cards: Discover, MasterCard, Visa
Personal Checks: Yes, with proper identification
Handicapped Accessible: No
Restaurants: Burger King
Bus Tours: Yes

Hingham

Gap
225 Lincoln (Route 3A)

Directions: One mile west of the Hingham rotary on Route 3A; or 2⁷⁄₁₀ miles west of Route 228 on Route 3A.
Phone: (617) 740–1022
Hours: 9:30 A.M.–9:00 P.M., Monday–Friday; 9:30 A.M.–6:00 P.M., Saturday; noon–5:00 P.M., Sunday
Credit Cards: American Express, Discover, MasterCard, Visa
Personal Checks: Yes, with proper identification
Handicapped Accessible: Yes
Bus Tours: No

Talbots
209 Lincoln (Route 3A)

Directions: One mile west of the Hingham rotary on Route 3A; or 2⁷⁄₁₀ miles west of Route 228 on Route 3A.
Phone: (617) 749–8720
Hours: 9:30 A.M.–9:00 P.M., Monday–Friday; 9:30 A.M.–6:00 P.M., Saturday; noon–5:00 P.M., Sunday

Credit Cards: American Express, MasterCard, Talbots Charge, Visa
Personal Checks: Yes, with proper identification
Handicapped Accessible: Yes
Bus Tours: No

Holliston

Creative Playthings
91 Washington Street

Directions: Washington Street is Route 16.
Phone: (508) 429–3888
Hours: 10:00 A.M.–6:00 P.M., Monday–Saturday; noon–5:00 P.M., Sunday
Credit Cards: MasterCard, Visa
Personal Checks: Yes, with proper identification
Handicapped Accessible: Yes
Bus Tours: Yes

Hyannis

Dansk
990 Route 132

Directions: From Route 6 take exit 6, Route 132 South, 2 miles into Hyannis. Dansk is on left.
Phone: (508) 775–3118
Hours: Open seven days a week; call ahead
Credit Cards: MasterCard, Visa
Personal Checks: Yes, with proper identification
Handicapped Accessible: Yes
Bus Tours: Yes

Lawrence

Hy-Sil Manufacturing, Gift Wrap Company of America
250 Canal Street

Directions: From I–95 take exit 45, Marston Street. Follow sign to downtown Lawrence. Take quick left onto Canal Street. Across from Everitt Mill.
Phone: (508) 689–2412
Hours: Mid-October to Christmas only: 8:30 A.M.–4:15 P.M., Monday–Friday; 9:00 A.M.–4:00 P.M., Saturday
Credit Cards: No
Personal Checks: No

New Balance
5 South Union Street

Directions: From I–495 North, take exit 43, Massachusetts Avenue. Go left at ramp, left at fork, right at lights onto South Union Street. Store is approximately 1½ blocks on left. From I–495 South, take exit 44, Sutton and Merrimac streets. Go right at ramp, right again at second set of lights onto South Union Street.
Phone: (508) 682–8960
Hours: 9:30 A.M.–5:00 P.M., Monday–Wednesday; 9:30 A.M.–7:00 P.M., Thursday; 9:30 A.M.–6:00 P.M., Friday–Saturday; noon–5:00 P.M., Sunday
Credit Cards: American Express, MasterCard, Visa
Personal Checks: Yes, with proper identification
Handicapped Accessible: No
Bus Tours: No

Lenox

Lenox House Country Shops
95 Pittsfield-Lenox Road

Directions: Follow Route 7 or Route 20.
Phone: No central phone number
Hours: 9:00 A.M.–6:00 P.M., Monday–Wednesday and Saturday; 9:00 A.M.–9:00 P.M., Thursday–Friday; noon–6:00 P.M., Sunday
Outlets:
Banister
Bass Shoe
Boston Traders
Corning/Revere
harvé benard
Leather Loft
L'eggs/Hanes/Bali
Manhattan
Van Heusen
Note: These shops will remind you of a New England village. Most, but not all, are outlets.

Littleton

Veryfine
Harvard Road

Directions: From Route 2 take the Taylor Street exit. Follow sign to Littleton. Take Taylor Street to Harvard Road.
Phone: (508) 692–0030
Hours: 8:00 A.M.–4:15 P.M., Monday–Friday
Credit Cards: No
Personal Checks: Yes, with proper identification
Handicapped Accessible: Yes
Bus Tours: Yes
Features: Factory tours are available with advance notice; call ahead to the personnel department.

Malden

Converse
35 Highland Avenue

Directions: Follow Highland Avenue into Malden to the store behind Caldor's Shopping Mall.
Phone: (617) 322–1500
Hours: 9:30 A.M.–9:00 P.M., Monday–Friday; 9:30 A.M.–8:00 P.M., Saturday; noon–5:00 P.M., Sunday
Credit Cards: American Express, MasterCard, Visa
Personal Checks: Yes, with proper identification
Handicapped Accessible: No
Restaurants: Burger King
Bus Tours: Yes

Marlborough

Rockport Shoe
Route 85

Directions: Exit 24 off I–495 to Route 20.
Phone: (508) 485–4752
Hours: 10:00 A.M.–6:00 P.M., Monday–Friday; 9:00 A.M.–5:00 P.M., Saturday; noon–5:00 P.M., Sunday
Credit Cards: American Express, MasterCard, Visa
Personal Checks: Yes, with proper identification
Handicapped Accessible: Yes

Remember that outlets accepting personal checks usually require at least two forms of proper identification, usually a driver's license and a major credit card.

Marshfield

Curtain Factory Outlet
Routes 139 and 3A

Directions: Exit 12 off Route 3 to Route 139.
Phone: (617) 834–4796
Hours: 9:30 A.M.–5:00 P.M., Monday–Wednesday and Friday–Saturday;
9:30 A.M.–8:00 P.M., Thursday; noon–5:00 P.M., Sunday
Credit Cards: Discover, MasterCard, Visa
Personal Checks: Yes, with proper identification
Handicapped Accessible: Yes
Bus Tours: Yes

Medfield

Pepperidge Farm
16 North Meadow Road

Directions: Call ahead.
Phone: (508) 359–8310
Hours: 9:30 A.M.–5:30 P.M., Monday–Saturday; noon–5:00 P.M., Sunday
Credit Cards: No
Personal Checks: Yes, United States, with proper identification
Handicapped Accessible: Yes
Bus Tours: Yes

Middleton

Pepperidge Farm
221 South Main Street

Directions: Call ahead.
Phone: (617) 774–6360
Hours: 9:00 A.M.–6:00 P.M., Monday–Friday; 9:00 A.M.–5:00 P.M., Saturday; noon–4:00 P.M., Sunday
Credit Cards: No

Personal Checks: Yes, United States, with proper identification
Handicapped Accessible: No
Bus Tours: Yes

Natick

Dan Howard's Maternity Factory Outlet
1298 East Worcester Road

Directions: Exit 13 off Massachusetts Turnpike, left after toll booth.
Right at first light. Right at sign for Route 9 West. Left at first light to
Sherwood Plaza.
Phone: (508) 653–4722
Hours: 10:00 A.M.–9:00 P.M., Monday and Thursday; 10:00 A.M.–6:00 P.M.,
Tuesday–Wednesday and Friday–Saturday; noon–5:00 P.M., Sunday
Credit Cards: American Express, Discover, MasterCard, Visa
Personal Checks: Yes, with proper identification
Handicapped Accessible: Yes
Bus Tours: Yes

New Bedford

Howland Place
651 Orchard Street

Directions: Take I–95 to exit 15, Route 18 South. At fourth traffic light,
turn right on Cove Road. At third traffic light, turn right on Orchard
Street. Howland Place is on the left.
Phone: (800) 327–SHOP (327–7467)
Hours: 10:00 A.M.–6:00 P.M., Monday–Wednesday and Saturday; 10:00
A.M.–9:00 P.M., Thursday; noon–6:00 P.M., Sunday; extended seasonal
hours
Features: This is one of the country's few large outlet centers devoted
to designers only. It is housed in a renovated mill.
Handicapped Accessible: Yes

Outlets:
Alessi & Bourgeat
Anne Klein
Bass
Bidermann
Calvin Klein
Eagle's Eye
First Choice
harvé benard
HE-RO Group
Jones New York
Libbey Glass
Mainely Bags
Moda
Mondi
9 West
Putamayo
Royal Doulton

WorleyBeds
197 Popes Island

Directions: Exit 15 off I–95. Call ahead for specifics.
Phone: (508) 997–6791
Hours: 9:00 A.M.–6:00 P.M., Monday–Friday; 9:00 A.M.–5:00 P.M., Saturday; closed Sunday
Credit Cards: American Express, Discover, MasterCard, Visa
Handicapped Accessible: Yes
Restaurants: Yes
Bus Tours: Yes

Newton

China Fair Warehouse
70 Needham Street

Directions: Needham Street, exit 19A off I–95.
Phone: (617) 332–1250
Hours: 9:00 A.M.–5:00 P.M., Monday–Saturday
Credit Cards: No
Personal Checks: Yes, Massachusetts, with proper identification
Handicapped Accessible: Yes, at rear entrance
Bus Tours: Yes

North Attleboro

Whiting and Davis
200 John Bietsch Boulevard

Directions: Take I–95 to exit 5. Call ahead for specifics.
Phone: (508) 699–4411
Hours: Noon–5:00 P.M., Monday–Friday; 9:00 A.M.–5:00 P.M., Saturday;
extended holiday hours
Credit Cards: MasterCard, Visa
Personal Checks: Yes, with proper identification
Handicapped Accessible: Yes
Bus Tours: Yes

North Dartmouth

Gaspar's Sausage
384 Faunce Corner Road

Directions: Call ahead.
Phone: (508) 998–2012
Hours: 8:00 A.M.–4:00 P.M., Monday–Friday; 8:00 A.M.–noon, Saturday

Credit Cards: MasterCard, Visa
Personal Checks: Yes, with proper identification
Handicapped Accessible: Yes
Bus Tours: Yes, by appointment

V. F. Factory Outlet Mall
375 Faunce Corner Road

Directions: Take I–95 to I–195 to exit 12B, Faunce Corner Road, North Dartmouth exit.
Phone: (508) 998–3311
Hours: 9:00 A.M.–9:00 P.M., Monday–Friday; 8:00 A.M.–9:00 P.M., Saturday; noon–5:00 P.M., Sunday
Features: Since 1970 Vanity Fair, the hub store, has been selling mill overruns and slight irregulars.
Personal Checks: Yes, with proper identification
Credit Cards: Discover, Mastercard, Visa
Bus Tours: Yes
Outlets:
American Tourister
Banister Shoe
Bass
Black & Decker
Bon Worth
Cape Isle Knitters
Famous Brands Housewares
Fieldcrest/Cannon
Jonathan Logan
Paper Factory
Prestige Fragrance and Cosmetics
Van Heusen
V. F. Outlet

North Oxford

North Oxford Mills
Clara Barton Road

Directions: Clara Barton Road is Route 12.
Phone: (508) 987–8521
Hours: 9:00 A.M.–5:00 P.M., Monday–Tuesday and Thursday–Saturday; 9:00 A.M.–9:00 P.M., Wednesday; closed Sunday
Credit Cards: MasterCard, Visa
Personal Checks: Yes, with proper identification
Handicapped Accessible: Yes
Restaurants: No
Bus Tours: Yes

Northbridge

Curtain Factory Outlet
2400 Providence Road

Directions: Route 122 off the Massachusetts Turnpike or Route 146 to the store.
Phone: (508) 234–2944
Hours: 9:30 A.M.–5:00 P.M., Monday–Saturday; noon–5:00 P.M., Sunday
Credit Cards: MasterCard, Visa
Personal Checks: Yes, with proper identification
Handicapped Accessible: Yes
Restaurants: No
Bus Tours: Yes

Norwell

Pepperidge Farm
340 Washington Street

Directions: Washington Street is Route 53.

Phone: (617) 659–1298
Hours: 9:00 A.M.–6:00 P.M., Monday–Friday; 9:00 A.M.–5:00 P.M., Saturday; noon–4:00 P.M., Sunday
Credit Cards: No
Personal Checks: Yes, United States, with proper identification
Handicapped Accessible: No
Bus Tours: No

WearGuard
Assinippi Industrial Park
141 Longwater Drive

Directions: Take Route 3 to exit 14, Route 228. Take entrance to Assinippi Industrial Park next to Boston Whaler. Factory Store is on the left, at rear of WearGuard corporate offices.
Phone: (800) 388–3300
Hours: 9:00 A.M.–9:00 P.M., Monday–Friday; 9:00 A.M.–5:00 P.M., Saturday; noon–5:00 P.M., Sunday
Credit Cards: American Express, Discover, MasterCard, Visa
Personal Checks: Yes, with proper identification
Handicapped Accessible: Yes
Bus Tours: Call ahead

Norwood

Entemann's Bakery
105–107 Providence Highway

Directions: Providence Highway is Route 1 South.
Phone: (617) 769–6635
Hours: 8:30 A.M.–6:00 P.M., Monday–Wednesday and Saturday–Sunday; 8:30 A.M.–8:00 P.M., Thursday–Friday
Credit Cards: No
Personal Checks: No
Handicapped Accessible: Yes
Bus Tours: Yes

Pembroke

E. T. Wright
Christmas Tree Plaza

Directions: Route 3 from north or south to exit 12. Plaza is at the intersection of Route 3 and 139.
Phone: (800) 846–9136
Hours: 9:00 A.M.–6:00 P.M., Monday–Wednesday and Saturday; 9:00 A.M.–8:00 P.M., Thursday and Friday; noon–5:00 P.M., Sunday
Credit Cards: American Express, Discover, MasterCard, Visa
Personal Checks: Yes, with proper identification
Handicapped Accessible: Yes
Bus Tours: No

Raynham

Curtain Factory Outlet
770 Broadway

Directions: Broadway is Route 138.
Phone: (508) 823–4196
Hours: 9:30 A.M.–5:00 P.M., Monday–Wednesday and Saturday; 9:30 a.m–8:00 P.M., Thursday and Friday; noon–5:00 P.M., Sunday
Credit Cards: Discover, MasterCard, Visa
Personal Checks: Yes, with proper identification
Handicapped Accessible: Yes
Bus Tours: Yes

Massachusetts

Reading

Frugal Fannie's
General Avenue

Directions: Take Route 128 to exit 39, North Avenue. Proceed toward Reading, ¼ mile. At Exxon station, turn left onto General Avenue in the 128 Industrial Park.
Phone: (617) 942–2121
Hours: Typically 8:00 A.M.–6:00 P.M., Saturday, and noon–5:00 P.M., Sunday. Closed for vacation from around July 4 to just before Labor Day. Always call ahead. A recorded message gives current hours.
Additional Savings: Twice-a-year Clean Sweep; annual coat, suit, separates sales. Mailing list.
Credit Cards: Discover, MasterCard, Visa
Personal Checks: Yes, with proper identification
Handicapped Accessible: No

Revere

Hy-Sil Manufacturing, Gift Wrap Company of America
28 Spring Avenue

Directions: Call ahead.
Phone: (617) 284–6000
Hours: 8:30 A.M.–4:15 P.M., Monday–Friday; 9:00 A.M.–4:00 P.M., Saturday; closed Sunday
Credit Cards: No
Personal Checks: No
Handicapped Accessible: Yes
Bus Tours: Yes, by prior arrangement

Sagamore

Cape Cod Factory Outlet Mall
Factory Outlet Road

Directions: Off Route 6, exit 1.
Phone: (508) 888–8417
Hours: 9:30 A.M.–9:00 P.M., Monday–Saturday; noon–6:00 P.M., Sunday
Handicapped Accessible: Yes
Restaurants: Sbarro, The Puppy Parlor, and several stands
Bus Tours: Yes
Attractions: Sagamore, on the Cape Cod side of the Sagamore Bridge, is not far from the Sandwich Glass Museum and Heritage Plantation.
Outlets:
Aileen
American Tourister
Banister Shoe
Bass
Bed & Bath
Bugle Boy
Carter's
Champion/Hanes
Colonial Candle of Cape Cod
Corning/Revere
Genuine Kids
Izod/Gant
L'eggs/Hanes/Bali
London Fog
OshKosh B'Gosh
Van Heusen

Pairpoint Glass Company
851 Sandwich Road

Directions: Route 6A is Sandwich Road.
Phone: (800) 899–0953

Hours: 8:00 A.M.–6:00 P.M., Monday–Saturday; 10:00 A.M.–6:00 P.M., Sunday
Credit Cards: American Express, Discover, MasterCard, Visa
Personal Checks: Yes, with proper identification
Handicapped Accessible: Yes
Restaurants: No
Bus Tours: Yes
Features: You can view glassblowing demonstrations weekdays, 9:00 A.M.–4:30 P.M.

Saugus

Dan Howard's Maternity Factory Outlet
Route 1

Directions: Route 1 North to Augustine's Plaza.
Phone: (617) 233–5254
Hours: 10:00 A.M.–9:00 P.M., Monday and Thursday; 10:00 A.M.–6:00 P.M., Tuesday–Wednesday and Friday–Saturday; noon–5:00 P.M., Sunday
Credit Cards: American Express, Discover, MasterCard, Visa
Personal Checks: Yes, with proper identification
Handicapped Accessible: Yes
Restaurants: Augustine's
Bus Tours: Yes

Seekonk

Pepperidge Farm
1397 Fall River Avenue (Route 6)

Directions: Call ahead.
Phone: (508) 336–5020
Hours: 9:30 A.M.–6:00 P.M., Monday–Friday; 9:30 A.M.–5:00 P.M., Saturday; noon–4:00 P.M. Sunday
Credit Cards: No

Personal Checks: Yes, United States, with proper identification
Handicapped Accessible: Yes
Bus Tours: No

South Deerfield

Yankee Candle
Routes 5 and 10

Directions: Exit 24 off I–91 North, turn right. Store is on the left.
Phone: (413) 665–8306
Hours: 9:30 A.M.–6:00 P.M., Monday–Sunday
Credit Cards: American Express, Discover, MasterCard, Visa
Personal Checks: Yes, with proper identification
Handicapped Accessible: Yes
Bus Tours: Yes

Springfield

Janlynn
40 Front Street

Directions: Located in the Indian Orchard section of Springfield.
Phone: (413) 543–3091
Hours: 10:00 A.M.–2:00 P.M., Tuesday–Friday
Credit Cards: MasterCard, Visa
Personal Checks: Yes, with proper identification
Handicapped Accessible: Yes
Bus Tours: No

Stoughton

Reebok/Rockport
300 Technology Drive

Directions: Located near the junction of Routes 24 and 139. Take exit 20A off Route 24; take a right at Stoughton Technology Center by the first set of lights.
Phone: (617) 341–4600
Hours: 10:00 A.M.–9:00 P.M., Monday–Friday; 9:00 A.M.–9:00 P.M., Saturday; noon–6:00 P.M. Sunday
Credit Cards: American Express, MasterCard, Visa
Personal Checks: Yes, to $300 maximum, with proper identification
Handicapped Accessible: Yes
Bus Tours: Yes

Twin-Kee Clothing
720 Park Street

Directions: Exit 18B off Route 24 onto Route 27 (Park Street).
Phone: (617) 344–4751
Hours: 10:00 A.M.–4:00 P.M., Monday–Saturday
Credit Cards: No
Personal Checks: Yes, with proper identification
Handicapped Accessible: Yes
Restaurants: Burger King
Bus Tours: Yes

Sturbridge

Sturbridge Country Village
420 Main Street

Directions: Take Route 20, west of Old Sturbridge Village.
Phone: (508) 347–9140
Hours: 10:00 A.M.–6:00 P.M., Monday–Sunday

Handicapped Accessible: Yes
Attractions: Close to Old Sturbridge Village, a historical reconstruction of a typical New England country town, with costumed interpreters in houses, mills, shops, crafts, and gardens.
Outlets:
Bass
Cape Isle Knitters
Just Coats and Swimwear
Van Heusen

Taunton

Reed and Barton Silversmiths
200 West Brittania Street

Directions: Route I–495 to Route 138 South. Call (800) 822–1824 for directions.
Phone: (508) 824–0289
Hours: 10:00 A.M.–6:00 P.M., Monday–Saturday
Credit Cards: MasterCard, Visa
Personal Checks: Yes, with proper identification
Handicapped Accessible: Yes
Bus Tours: Yes

Swank
656 Joseph Warner Boulevard

Directions: Route 24 to Route 44 to Joseph Warner Boulevard.
Phone: (508) 822–2527
Hours: 9:00 A.M.–5:00 P.M., Monday–Saturday; noon–5:00 P.M., Sunday; extended holiday hours
Credit Cards: Discover, MasterCard, Visa
Personal Checks: Yes, with proper identification
Handicapped Accessible: Yes
Restaurants: McDonald's
Bus Tours: Yes

Uxbridge

Uxbridge Yarn Mill
27 Mendon Street

Directions: Route 146 to Route 16.
Phone: (508) 278–7748
Hours: 9:30 A.M.–4:30 P.M., Monday–Saturday
Credit Cards: MasterCard, Visa
Personal Checks: Yes, with proper identification
Handicapped Accessible: No
Bus Tours: Yes

Ware

Curious Cargo
234 West Street

Directions: Exit 8 off Massachusetts Turnpike to Route 32 (West Street).
Phone: (413) 967–7976
Hours: 10:00 A.M.–5:00 P.M., Tuesday–Saturday
Credit Cards: American Express, Discover, MasterCard, Visa
Personal Checks: No
Handicapped Accessible: No
Bus Tours: Yes

Stone Mill Marketplace
Industry Yard
East Main Street, junction of Routes 9 and 32

Directions: Take Massachusetts Turnpike to Exit 8 to Route 32.
Phone: (413) 967–5964
Hours: 9:00 A.M.–5:00 P.M., Monday–Saturday; noon–5:00 P.M., Sunday
Handicapped Accessible: Yes
Bus Tours: Yes

Outlets:
American Home Sewing
Bag Outlet
Frederic's Mill
Ware Sports Wear

Westwood

Frugal Fannie's
24 Wilson Way

Directions: Take Route 128 to exit 15B, Route 1 South. Go 1 mile on Route 1 South. Turn right before McDonald's onto Glacier Drive. Follow Glacier ¼ mile to end at Wilson Way. Look for yellow awning.
Phone: (617) 329–8996
Hours: Typically 5:00–9:30 P.M., Friday; 7:00 A.M.–6:00 P.M., Saturday and 11:00 A.M.–6:00 P.M., Sunday. Closed for vacation from around July 4 to before Labor Day. Always call ahead; a recorded message gives current hours.
Additional Savings: Twice-a-year Clean Sweep; annual coat, suit, separates sales. Mailing list.
Credit Cards: Discover, MasterCard, Visa
Personal Checks: Yes, with proper identification
Handicapped Accessible: No

West Yarmouth

Cranberry Bog Factory Outlet Center
Route 28, West Yarmouth

Directions: Take Route 28 to West Yarmouth.
Phone: (508) 775–5536
Hours: 9:00 A.M.–6:00 P.M., Monday–Thursday; 9:00 A.M.–9:00 P.M., Friday–Saturday; noon–6:00 P.M., Sunday

Outlets:
Aileen
Bass
Cape Isle Knitters
Van Heusen

Winchendon

Winchendon Furniture
13 Railroad Street

Directions: Route 2 to Route 140 North. Take left on Route 12 North, turn right onto Central Street, and take third left onto Railroad Street.
Phone: (508) 297–0131
Hours: 9:00 A.M.–5:30 P.M., Monday–Wednesday and Saturday; 9:00 A.M.–8:00 P.M., Thursday–Friday; noon–5:00 P.M., Sunday
Credit Cards: Discover, MasterCard, Visa
Personal Checks: Yes, with proper identification
Handicapped Accessible: No
Bus Tours: Yes

Winthrop

Curtains Plus
Putnam Street

Directions: Route 1A to Route 145. Left on Walden Street to end. Take first left, then first right. The store is to the rear of McDonald's.
Phone: (617) 846–8066
Hours: 9:00 A.M.–5:30 P.M., Monday–Saturday
Credit Cards: American Express, Discover, MasterCard, Visa
Personal Checks: Yes, with proper identification
Handicapped Accessible: Yes
Restaurants: McDonald's, Brigham's
Bus Tours: Yes

Woburn

Crate & Barrel
460 Wildwood Street

Directions: Take Route 128 to exit 36. Take right off exit ramp, then right on Olympia. After ¾ mile, take left on Wildwood Street.
Phone: (617) 938–8777
Hours: 10:00 A.M.–5:00 P.M., Monday–Saturday
Credit Cards: American Express, Discover, MasterCard, Visa
Personal Checks: Yes, with proper identification
Handicapped Accessible: No
Bus Tours: No

Worcester

Don-Frederick Factory Outlet
108 Grove Street

Directions: Lincoln Square exit off Route 290.
Phone: (508) 755–3196
Hours: 10:00 A.M.–6:00 P.M., Monday–Friday; 10:00 A.M.–5:00 P.M., Saturday; noon–5:00 P.M., Sunday
Credit Cards: Discover, MasterCard, Visa
Personal Checks: Yes, with proper identification
Handicapped Accessible: Yes
Bus Tours: Yes

Worcester Common Fashion Outlets
100 Front Street

Directions: Take Route 290 to exit 16. Outlets are across from The Centrum.
Phone: (508) 798–2581 or (800) 2–SAVE–ALOT
Hours: 9:00 A.M.–9:00 P.M., Monday–Saturday; noon–6:00 P.M., Sunday
Handicapped Accessible: Yes; Complimentary wheelchairs available at

The Customer Service Center. Strollers available for $2.00/day.
Restaurants: Yes, a dozen in the Food Court
Features: Indoor parking is available for $ .99 for 3 hours with a $25.00 purchase.
Outlets:
Ann Taylor
Bag and Baggage
Barneys New York
Bass
Bed, Bath, and Beyond
Benetton
Boston Traders
B.U.M.
Colours by Alexander Julian
Donna Karan
Fila
Filene's Basement
Genuine Kids
Guess? Again
Joan & David
Jockey
Jones New York
Levi's
Lily of France
Lingerie Factory
London Fog
Maidenform
Mikasa
Miltons
9 West
OshKosh B'Gosh
Polo/Ralph Lauren
Saks Fifth Avenue Clearinghouse
Van Heusen
Westport, Ltd.

Worcester Tool
475 Shrewsbury Street

Directions: Exit 15 off Route 290 East onto Shrewsbury Street.
Phone: (508) 799–4111
Hours: 8:00 A.M.–6:00 P.M., Monday–Friday; 8:00 A.M.–5:00 P.M., Saturday
Credit Cards: American Express, Discover, MasterCard, Visa
Personal Checks: Yes, with proper identification
Handicapped Accessible: Yes
Bus Tours: Yes

---

*Can't remember what product a particular outlet offers? Check our
"Profiles" section beginning on page one. Many listings also contain
information on brand names and range of discounts.*

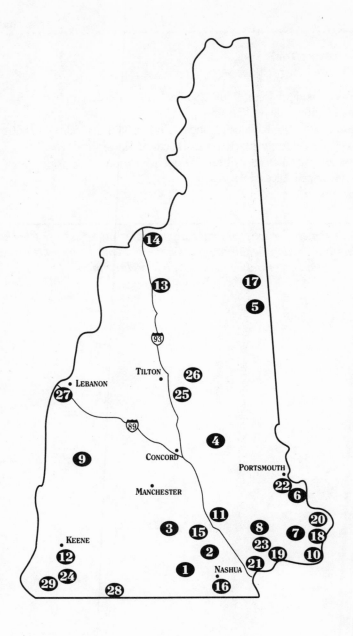

New Hampshire

Numbers at the left of this legend correspond to the numbers on the accompanying map. The number to the right of each city's or town's name is the page number on which that municipality's outlets first appear in this book.

1. Amherst, 138
2. Bedford, 138
3. Bradford, 139
4. Chichester, 139
5. Conway, 140
6. Dover, 141
7. Exeter, 141
8. Fremont, 141
9. Guild, 142
10. Hampton Falls, 142
11. Hooksett, 143
12. Keene, 143
13. Lincoln, 144
14. Littleton, 144
15. Manchester, 145

16. Nashua, 145
17. North Conway, 146
18. North Hampton, 151
19. Plaistow, 152
20. Portsmouth, 152
21. Salem, 153
22. Somersworth, 153
23. Stratham, 153
24. Swanzey, 154
25. Tilton, 154
26. Weirs Beach, 156
27. West Lebanon, 156
28. West Rindge, 157
29. West Swanzey, 157

Amherst

Dexter Shoe
Route 101A

Directions: From Everett Turnpike, take exit 8 West onto Route 101A West to Amherst.
Phone: (603) 883–1185
Hours: 10:00 A.M.–6:00 P.M., Monday–Wednesday; 10:00 A.M.–8:00 P.M., Thursday–Saturday; 11:00 A.M.–6:00 P.M., Sunday
Credit Cards: MasterCard, Visa
Personal Checks: Yes, with proper identification
Handicapped Accessible: Yes
Bus Tours: Yes

Winchendon Furniture
Route 101A

Directions: From Route 3 in Nashua, take Route 101A West 4 miles. Store is on right.
Phone: (603) 880–6393
Hours: 10:00 A.M.–6:00 P.M., Tuesday–Wednesday; 10:00 A.M.–8:00 P.M., Thursday–Friday; 10:00 A.M.–5:00 P.M., Saturday; 1:00–5:00 P.M., Sunday
Credit Cards: Discover, MasterCard, Visa
Personal Checks: Yes, with proper identification
Bus Tours: Yes

Bedford

Adams Mill
Route 101 West

Directions: From I–93 North, exit onto Route 101 West and proceed to the store.
Phone: (603) 472–3928
Hours: 10:00 A.M.–6:00 P.M., Monday–Sunday

Credit Cards: MasterCard, Visa
Personal Checks: Yes, with proper identification
Handicapped Accessible: Yes
Bus Tours: Yes

Bradford

Barns of Bradford
Route 114

Directions: Exit 5 off I–89, west on Route 202 to Henniker, north on Route 114 to store.
Phone: (603) 938–2618
Hours: 10:00 A.M.–5:00 P.M., Monday–Saturday; 11:00 A.M.–4:00 P.M., Sunday
Credit Cards: MasterCard, Visa
Personal Checks: Yes, with proper identification
Handicapped Accessible: Yes, first floor only
Bus Tours: Yes

Chichester

Dexter Shoe
Route 4 East

Directions: Directly off I–393 interchange.
Phone: (603) 225–5348
Hours: 9:30 A.M.–6:00 P.M., Monday–Thursday and Saturday; 9:30 A.M.–8:00 P.M., Friday; 10:30 A.M.–5:00 P.M., Sunday
Credit Cards: MasterCard, Visa
Personal Checks: Yes, with proper identification
Handicapped Accessible: Yes
Bus Tours: Yes

Conway

Conway Crossing
Junction Routes 16 and 153

Directions: Take Route 16 to intersection with Route 153.
Phone: No central phone number
Hours: Winter hours 10:00 A.M.–6:00 P.M., Monday–Saturday; 10:00 A.M.–5:00 P.M., Sunday. Summer hours 9:00 A.M.–9:00 P.M., Monday–Saturday; 10:00 A.M.–5:00 P.M., Sunday
Outlets:
Jonathan Logan
Leather Loft
Prestige Fragrance and Cosmetics

Reebok/Rockport
Conway Marketplace
Route 16

Directions: Call Ahead.
Phone: (603) 447–6994
Hours: 10:00 A.M.–6:00 P.M., Monday–Sunday
Credit Cards: MasterCard, Visa
Personal Checks: Yes, with proper identification

Dexter Shoe
Route 16

Directions: The store is ½ mile north of Conway Village.
Phone: (603) 447–2601
Hours: 9:00 A.M.–9:00 P.M., Monday–Saturday; 10:00 A.M.–8:00 P.M., Sunday
Credit Cards: MasterCard, Visa
Personal Checks: Yes, with proper identification
Handicapped Accessible: Yes
Bus Tours: Yes

Dover

Yield House
701 Central Avenue

Directions: Exit 9 North off I–95. After rotary bear right on Route 108. Pass through four sets of traffic lights. Store is ½ mile on the left.
Phone: (603) 749–3495
Hours: 10:00 A.M.–5:00 P.M., Monday–Saturday; noon–5:00 P.M., Sunday
Credit Cards: American Express, Discover, MasterCard, Visa, Yield House credit card
Handicapped Accessible: Yes
Bus Tours: Yes

Exeter

Exeter Handkerchief Company
48 Lincoln Street

Directions: Through Exeter business district on Water Street, left onto Lincoln Street.
Phone: (603) 778–8564
Hours: 9:00 A.M.–5:00 P.M., Monday–Saturday
Credit Cards: MasterCard, Visa
Personal Checks: Yes, with proper identification
Handicapped Accessible: Yes
Bus Tours: Yes

Fremont

Spaulding & Frost
326 Main Street

Directions: Route 107 to Route 1 or Route 107 to Fremont. Route 107 is Main Street.

Phone: (603) 895–4703
Hours: 11:00 A.M.–5:00 P.M., Saturday–Sunday. For other times, call
ahead.
Credit Cards: MasterCard, Visa
Personal Checks: Yes, with proper identification
Handicapped Accessible: Yes
Bus Tours: Yes

Guild

Dorr Mill Store
Routes 11 and 103

Directions: From I–89 take Route 11 to Route 103 intersection in
Guild.
Phone: (603) 863–1197
Hours: 9:00 A.M.–5:00 P.M., Monday–Saturday
Credit Cards: MasterCard, Visa
Personal Checks: Yes, with proper identification
Handicapped Accessible: Yes
Bus Tours: Yes

Hampton Falls

Dexter Shoe
Route 1 (Lafayette Road)

Directions: From I–95 take Seabrook exit (Route 107). The store is ap-
proximately 1 mile north on Route 1 (Lafayette Road).
Phone: (603) 926–2595
Hours: 9:00 A.M.–9:00 P.M., Monday–Saturday; 10:00 A.M.–6:00 P.M., Sun-
day; shorter winter hours
Credit Cards: MasterCard, Visa
Personal Checks: Yes, with proper identification
Handicapped Accessible: Yes
Bus Tours: Yes

Hooksett

Dexter Shoe
1329 Daniel Webster Highway (Hooksett Road)

Directions: Routes 3 and 28.
Phone: (603) 669–0672
Hours: 10:00 A.M.–6:00 P.M., Monday–Wednesday; 10:00 A.M.–8:00 P.M.,
Thursday–Saturday; 10:00 A.M.–6:00 P.M., Sunday; shorter winter hours
Credit Cards: MasterCard, Visa
Personal Checks: Yes, with proper identification
Handicapped Accessible: Yes
Bus Tours: Yes

Keene

Cuddle Toys by Douglas
The Center at Keene
149 Emerald Street

Directions: Follow Route 10 to Ralston Street. The center is at the end
of Ralston Street.
Phone: (603) 357–0823
Hours: 9:30 A.M.–5:00 P.M., Monday–Saturday
Credit Cards: MasterCard, Visa
Personal Checks: Yes, with proper identification
Handicapped Accessible: Yes
Bus Tours: Yes

Keene Mill End Store
55 Ralston Street

Directions: Ralston Street is off Winchester Street, past Keene State
College.
Phone: (603) 352–8683
Hours: 9:30 A.M.–5:30 P.M., Monday–Thursday and Saturday; 9:30
A.M.–9:00 P.M., Friday

Credit Cards: Discover, MasterCard, Visa
Personal Checks: Yes, with proper identification
Handicapped Accessible: Yes
Bus Tours: Yes

Lincoln

Bass
Lincoln Square
Corner of Maple and Main streets

Directions: Call ahead.
Phone: (603) 745–8949
Hours: 9:00 A.M.–9:00 P.M., Monday–Saturday; 10:00 a.m–6:00 P.M., Sunday
Credit Cards: American Express, Discover, MasterCard, Visa
Personal Checks: Yes, with proper identification
Handicapped Accessible: Yes

Littleton

Dexter Shoe
50 Meadow Street (Route 302)

Directions: The store is on Route 302 East, ½ mile from exit 42 off I–93.
Phone: (603) 444–6834
Hours: 10:00 A.M.–5:00 P.M., Monday–Sunday; longer summer hours
Credit Cards: MasterCard, Visa
Personal Checks: Yes, with proper identification
Handicapped Accessible: Yes
Bus Tours: Yes

Manchester

Dexter Shoe
2004 South Willow Street

Directions: From Route 101 take the South Willow Street exit. Go ⁹⁄₁₀ mile past the Mall of New Hampshire on Route 28 South.
Phone: (603) 622–7131
Hours: 9:30 A.M.–9:00 P.M., Monday–Saturday; 10:00 A.M.–6:00 P.M., Sunday
Credit Cards: MasterCard, Visa
Personal Checks: Yes, with proper identification
Handicapped Accessible: Yes, first floor only
Bus Tours: Yes

Nashua

Bass
531 Amherst Street (Route 101A)

Directions: Exit 8 off Route 3 (Everett Turnpike) onto Route 101A (Amherst Street).
Phone: (603) 889–6000
Hours: 9:00 A.M.–9:00 P.M., Monday–Saturday; 10:00 A.M.–6:00 P.M., Sunday
Credit Cards: Discover, MasterCard, Visa
Personal Checks: Yes, with proper identification
Handicapped Accessible: Yes
Bus Tours: Yes

Dexter Shoe
195 Daniel Webster Highway

Directions: From the Everett Turnpike take the Spit Brook Road Exit to the Daniel Webster Highway. The store is ½ mile north of the exit.

Phone: (603) 888–7855
Hours: 9:30 A.M.–9:00 P.M., Monday–Saturday; 10:00 A.M.–6:00 P.M., Sunday
Credit Cards: MasterCard, Visa
Personal Checks: Yes, with proper identification
Handicapped Accessible: Yes
Bus Tours: Yes

Pepperidge Farm
Market Place Shoppes
110–112 Daniel Webster Highway

Directions: From the Everett Turnpike take the Spit Brook Road exit to the Daniel Webster Highway.
Phone: (603) 888–2338
Hours: 9:30 A.M.–5:30 P.M., Monday–Friday; 9:30 A.M.–5:00 P.M., Saturday; 11:00 A.M.–3:00 P.M., Sunday
Credit Cards: No
Personal Checks: Yes, United States, with proper identification
Handicapped Accessible: Yes
Bus Tours: No

*North Conway

North Conway is not only a beautiful destination in the White Mountains for winter skiers and summer vacationers; it is one of the major outlet centers in New England. Outlet malls and outlets line Route 16. Also, you will find a variety of restaurants on Route 16.

Boston Traders/Genuine Kids
Route 16

Phone: (603) 356–2616
Hours: Summer: 10:00 a.m–9:00 P.M., Monday–Sunday. Winter: 10:00 A.M.–6:00 P.M., Monday–Thursday and Sunday; 10:00 A.M.–8:00 P.M., Friday–Saturday

Credit Cards: American Express, Discover, MasterCard, Visa
Personal Checks: Yes, with proper identification
Handicapped Accessible: Yes

Dansk
Route 16

Phone: (603) 356–3493
Hours: Summer: 9:00 A.M.–8:00 P.M., Monday–Saturday; 9:00 A.M.–5:00 P.M., Sunday; Winter: 9:30 A.M.–6:00 P.M., Monday–Thursday; 9:30 A.M.–8:00 P.M., Friday–Saturday; 9:00 A.M.–5:00 P.M., Sunday
Credit Cards: MasterCard, Visa
Personal Checks: Yes, with proper identification
Handicapped Accessible: No

Indian Head Village Plaza
Route 16

Phone: No central phone number
Hours: 9:30 A.M.–6:00 P.M., Monday–Saturday; 11:00 A.M.–5:00 P.M., Sunday
Outlets:
Danskin
Kitchen Collection

L.L. Bean Factory Store and Plaza
Route 16

Phone: (603) 356–2100
Hours: 9:00 A.M.–9:00 P.M., Monday–Saturday; 10:00 A.M.–6:00 P.M., Sunday; extended seasonal hours
Bus Tours: Yes
Outlets:
American Tourister
Anne Klein
Cole-Haan Shoes

Donna Karan
Fanny Farmer
Izod/Gant
Joan & David Shoes
L. L. Bean
Maidenform
Oneida

Mountain View Mall
Route 16

Phone: No central phone number
Hours: 10:00 A.M.–6:00 P.M., Monday–Sunday
Outlets:
L'eggs/Hanes/Bali

Mt. Washington Valley Factory Outlets
Route 16

Phone: No central phone number
Hours: 10:00 A.M.–6:00 P.M., Monday–Sunday
Outlets:
Chuck Roast
Le Sportsac
London Fog
Timberland

North Conway Factory Outlet Center
Route 16

Phone: No central phone number
Hours: 9:30 A.M.–6:00 P.M., Sunday–Thursday; 9:30 A.M.–8:00 P.M., Friday–Saturday
Outlets:
Pfaltzgraff
Swank

Red Barn Factory Stores
Route 16

Phone: (603) 356–7921
Hours: 10:00 A.M.–6:00 P.M., Monday–Sunday; extended seasonal hours
Outlets:
Banister Shoe
Casual Corner
Champion/Hanes
Corning/Revere
Easy Spirit
John Henry & Friends
OshKosh B'Gosh
Socks Galore and More
totes
Wallet Works

Red Pines Shopping Center
Route 16

Phone: No central phone number
Hours: 10:00 A.M.–6:00 P.M., Monday–Sunday; extended seasonal hours
Handicapped Accessible: Yes
Outlets:
Polly Flinders

Settlers' Green Outlet Village Plus
Route 16

Directions: North of Route 302 on Route 16.
Phone: (603) 356–7031
Hours: 10:00 A.M.–6:00 P.M., Monday–Saturday; 10:00 A.M.–5:00 P.M., Sunday
Outlets:
Barbizon Lingerie
Eddie Bauer
J. Crew

Seiko
Yankee Candle
Features: Mix of retail shops, outlets, and a hotel in a village setting
Handicapped Accessible: Yes
Restaurants: Yes, five in complex
Bus Tours: Yes

Tanger Factory Outlet Center
Route 16

Phone: (603) 356–7921
Hours: 10:00 A.M.–6:00 P.M., Monday–Thursday and Sunday: 10:00
A.M.–9:00 P.M., Friday–Saturday; some outlets have extended hours
Outlets:
Calvin Klein
Coloratura
Liz Claiborne
Polo/Ralph Lauren

Willow Place
Route 16

Directions: Call ahead.
Phone: No central phone number
Hours: 10:00 A.M.–6:00 P.M., Monday–Thursday and Sunday; 10:00
A.M.–8:00 P.M., Friday–Saturday
Outlets:
Bed & Bath
Casual Male
Leather Outpost
Lingerie Factory Outlet
Toys Unlimited

North Hampton

Dexter Shoe
Route 1

Directions: The store is on Route 1, between Rye Beach and Hampton Beach.
Phone: (603) 964–5513
Hours: 10:00 A.M.–9:00 P.M., Monday–Saturday; 10:30 A.M.–5:30 P.M., Sunday
Credit Cards: MasterCard, Visa
Personal Checks: Yes, with proper identification
Handicapped Accessible: Yes
Bus Tours: Yes

North Hampton Factory Outlet Center
Route 1, Lafayette Road

Phone: (603) 964–9050
Hours: 10:00 A.M.–9:00 P.M., Monday–Saturday; 10:00 A.M.–6:00 P.M., Sunday
Outlets:
Aileen
American Tourister
Bass
Bed & Bath
Book and Music Outlet
Famous Footwear
Kitchen Etc.
Leather Outpost
Lingerie Factory Outlet
Paper Factory
Polly Flinders
Van Heusen
Welcome Home

Plaistow

Dexter Shoe
Route 125

Directions: Route 495 to Route 125, north to Plaistow.
Phone: (603) 382–5144
Hours: 10:00 A.M.–8:00 P.M., Monday–Saturday; 10:00 A.M.–6:00 P.M., Sunday; shorter winter hours
Credit Cards: MasterCard, Visa
Personal Checks: Yes, with proper identification
Handicapped Accessible: Yes
Restaurants: Wendy's
Bus Tours: Yes

Portsmouth

The Artisan Outlet
72 Mirona Road

Directions: Take exit 5 off I–95 to Route 1 South; proceed 2 miles south of the Portsmouth Circle to Mirona Road on right.
Phone: (603) 436–0022
Hours: 9:30 A.M.–9:00 P.M., Monday–Saturday; noon–5:00 P.M., Sunday; shorter winter hours
Credit Cards: Artisan Outlet credit card, Discover, MasterCard, Visa
Personal Checks: Yes, with proper identification
Handicapped Accessible: Yes
Bus Tours: Yes
Attractions: Visit historic Strawbery Banke, a beautifully restored eighteenth-century neighborhood, while in the Portsmouth area.
Outlets:
Artisan Outlet
Lindt of Switzerland

Salem

Dexter Shoe
Route 28

Directions: The store is ¾ mile north of Rockingham Park.
Phone: (603) 898–4001
Hours: 10:00 A.M.–9:00 P.M., Monday–Saturday; 11:00 A.M.–6:00 P.M., Sunday
Credit Cards: MasterCard, Visa
Personal Checks: Yes, with proper identification
Handicapped Accessible: Yes
Bus Tours: Yes

Somersworth

Russell Stover
Malley Farm Business Center

Directions: Take exit 9 off Route 6, Spaulding Highway.
Phone: (603) 692–2044
Hours: 9:00 A.M.–5:00 P.M., Monday–Saturday; noon–5:00 P.M., Sunday
Credit Cards: MasterCard, Visa
Personal Checks: Yes, with proper identification
Handicapped Accessible: Yes

Stratham

Lindt of Switzerland
Stratham Industrial Park
One Fine Chocolate Place

Directions: Take I–95 to exit 2, Route 51. Continue on Route 51 West 1 mile to Route 111 exit. First left is Stratham Industrial Park. Factory is at end of drive.
Phone: (603) 778–8100
Hours: 9:30 A.M.–6:00 P.M., Monday–Friday

Credit Cards: MasterCard, Visa
Personal Checks: Yes, with proper identification
Handicapped Accessible: Yes
Bus Tours: Yes

Swanzey

Dexter Shoe
Route 12

Directions: The store is on Route 12, 2 miles south of the Route 12 and Route 101 junction.
Phone: (603) 352–0055
Hours: 9:30 A.M.–6:00 P.M., Monday–Thursday; 9:30 A.M.–8:00 P.M., Friday; 9:30 A.M.–7:00 P.M., Saturday; 10:00 A.M.–6:00 P.M., Sunday; shorter winter hours
Credit Cards: MasterCard, Visa
Personal Checks: Yes, with proper identification
Handicapped Accessible: Yes
Bus Tours: Yes

Tilton

Lakes Region Factory Stores
Route 3

Directions: Take exit 20 off I–93. Outlet is on the north side of Route 3, east of Route 93.
Phone: (603) 286–7880
Hours: 9:00 A.M.–9:00 P.M., Monday–Saturday; 11:00 A.M.–6:00 P.M., Sunday
Handicapped Accessible: Yes
Outlets:
Bass
Big Dog
Book Warehouse
Brooks Brothers

B.U.M.
Cape Isle Knitters
Carter's
Casual Corner
Champion/Hanes
Chicago Cutlery
Chuck Roast
Coach
Corning/Revere
Eagle's Eye
Easy Spirit
Famous Brands Housewares
Farberware
Fila
Florsheim
Genuine Kids
Geoffrey Beene
Hush Puppies
J. Crew
Jockey
John Henry and Friends
Kitchen Collection/Proctor-Silex/Wearever
Leather Loft
L'eggs/Hanes/Bali
Leslie Fay
Levi's
London Fog
Maidenform
Mikasa
9 West
OshKosh B'Gosh
Paper Factory
Polo/Ralph Lauren
Prestige Fragrance and Cosmetics
totes
Van Heusen
Welcome Home
Westport, Ltd.

Weirs Beach

Dexter Shoe
Dexter Village at Weirs

Directions: Junction of Routes 3 and 11B.
Phone: (603) 366–5111
Hours: 9:30 A.M.–6:00 P.M., Monday–Thursday; 9:30 A.M.–8:00 P.M., Friday–Saturday; 10:00 A.M.–6:00 P.M., Sunday
Credit Cards: MasterCard, Visa
Personal Checks: Yes, with proper identification
Handicapped Accessible: Yes
Bus Tours: Yes

West Lebanon

Bass
Colonial Plaza Shopping Center
Route 12A

Directions: I–91 to Route 89 south, take exit 20 off 89. At bottom of exit take a right to go south on Route 12A, take a left onto Airport Road to Colonial Shopping Center.
Phone: (603) 298–8044
Hours: 9:00 A.M.–9:00 P.M., Monday–Saturday; 10:00 A.M.–6:00 P.M., Sunday
Credit Cards: Discover, MasterCard, Visa
Personal Checks: Yes, with proper identification
Handicapped Accessible: Yes

Dexter Shoe
South Main Street

Directions: Exit 20 off I–89.
Phone: (603) 298–5290
Hours: 9:30 A.M.–8:00 P.M., Monday–Thursday; 9:30 A.M.–9:00 P.M., Friday; 9:30 A.M.–8:00 P.M., Saturday; noon–6:00 P.M., Sunday

Credit Cards: MasterCard, Visa
Personal Checks: Yes, with proper identification
Handicapped Accessible: Yes
Bus Tours: Yes

West Rindge

West Rindge Baskets
Main Street

Directions: The store is off Route 202, in West Rindge Village.
Phone: (603) 899–2231
Hours: 8:00 A.M.–4:00 P.M., Monday–Thursday; 10:00 A.M.–4:00 P.M., Friday and Saturday
Credit Cards: No
Personal Checks: Yes, with proper identification
Handicapped Accessible: No
Bus Tours: Yes

West Swanzey

Homestead Woolen Mill
Winchester Street

Directions: Route 10 to Winchester Street.
Phone: (603) 352–2022
Hours: 9:00 A.M.–4:00 P.M., Tuesday–Friday; 9:00 A.M.–noon, Saturday
Credit Cards: MasterCard, Visa
Personal Checks: Yes, with proper identification
Handicapped Accessible: No
Bus Tours: Yes

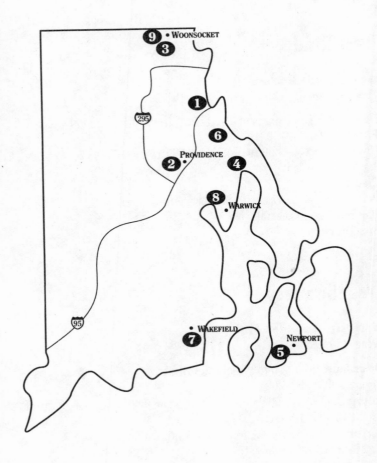

WOONSOCKET

PROVIDENCE

WARWICK

WAKEFIELD

NEWPORT

Rhode Island

Numbers at the left of this legend correspond to the numbers on the accompanying map. The number to the right of each city's or town's name is the page number on which that municipality's outlets first appear in this book.

NOTE: In Rhode Island you're not far from factory outlets in Mystic, Connecticut, and Fall River and New Bedford, Massachusetts.

Central Falls

American Broadloom Braided Rug and Furniture Company
414 Roosevelt Avenue

Directions: Take exit 30 from I–95.
Phone: (401) 722–2017
Hours: 9:00 A.M.–5:00 P.M., Monday, Wednesday, and Saturday; 9:00 A.M.–9:00 P.M., Tuesday, Thursday, and Friday; noon–5:00 P.M., Sunday
Credit Cards: MasterCard, Visa
Personal Checks: Yes, with proper identification
Handicapped Accessible: Yes
Bus Tours: Yes

Providence Yarn
280 Rand Street

Directions: From North: I–95 to exit 30. Go parallel to highway to second set of lights. Turn right onto Central Street, which becomes Cove Street. Follow Cove to end. Turn right onto Pine. First street on left is Rand. From South: I–95 to exit 26, Lonsdale Avenue. At traffic light turn left and proceed 1 mile. Take right on Rand Street.
Phone: (401) 722–5600
Hours: 9:00 A.M.–4:30 P.M., Monday–Friday; 9:00 A.M.–1:00 P.M., Saturday; closed Saturday in summer
Credit Cards: MasterCard, Visa
Personal Checks: Yes, with proper identification
Handicapped Accessible: No
Bus Tours: Yes

Cranston

Two's Company
1550 Elmwood Avenue

Directions: Exit 17 off I–95. Proceed south on Elmwood Avenue

Phone: (401) 781–2222
Hours: 9:00 A.M.–5:00 P.M., Monday–Friday
Credit Cards: MasterCard, Visa
Personal Checks: Yes, with proper identification
Handicapped Accessible: Yes
Bus Tours: Yes

Cumberland

Slater Fabrics
2 Industrial Way

Directions: Take exit 11 off I–295.
Phone: (401) 727–9068
Hours: 10:00 A.M.–5:00 P.M., Monday–Friday; 10:00 A.M.–2:00 P.M., Saturday
Credit Cards: No
Personal Checks: No
Handicapped Accessible: Yes
Bus Tours: Yes

East Providence

Entemann's Bakery
290 Newport Avenue

Directions: Newport Avenue is Route 1A.
Phone: (401) 434–1719
Hours: 9:00 A.M.–5:00 P.M., Monday and Saturday–Sunday; 9:00 A.M.–6:00 P.M., Tuesday–Friday
Credit Cards: No
Personal Checks: No
Handicapped Accessible: Yes
Bus Tours: Yes

Newport

Note: Newport is probably better known for millionaires than outlets. But this charming town is worth a stop for lunch. Be warned, however, that traffic moves very slowly in the summer. If you're going to stop, give yourself extra time.

Cole-Haan Shoes
206 Bellevue Avenue

Directions: Next to the Tennis Hall of Fame.
Phone: (401) 846–4906
Hours: 9:00 A.M.–6:00 P.M., Monday–Saturday; 11:00 A.M.–6:00 P.M., Sunday
Credit Cards: American Express, MasterCard, Visa
Personal Checks: Yes, with proper identification
Handicapped Accessible: No
Bus Tours: No

Pawtucket

Lorraine Mill Fabrics
593 Mineral Spring Avenue

Directions: From North: I–95 to exit 27. Take right onto Pine Street, left onto Main Street, right onto Mineral Spring Avenue. From South: I–95 to exit 25 onto Smithfield Avenue and right onto Mineral Spring Avenue.
Phone: (401) 722–9500
Hours: 10:00 A.M.–6:00 P.M., Tuesday–Saturday; noon–5:00 P.M., Sunday
Credit Cards: MasterCard, Visa
Personal Checks: Yes, with proper identification
Handicapped Accessible: No
Restaurants: McDonald's
Bus Tours: Yes

Rug Factory
560 Mineral Spring Avenue

Directions: From North: I–95 to exit 27. Take right onto Pine Street, left onto Main Street, right onto Mineral Spring Avenue. From South: I–95 to exit 25 onto Smithfield Avenue and right onto Mineral Spring Avenue.
Phone: (401) 724–6840
Hours: 9:00 A.M.–5:00 P.M., Monday–Wednesday, Friday–Saturday; 9:00 A.M. to 9:00 P.M., Tuesday and Thursday; noon–5:00 P.M., Sunday
Credit Cards: Discover, MasterCard, Visa
Personal Checks: Yes, with proper identification
Handicapped Accessible: No
Bus Tours: Yes

Textile Warehouse
Corner of Division Street and Industrial Highway

Directions: Exit 27 from I–95 North; right at third traffic light to first left onto Division. Or, exit 27 from I–95 South; left at traffic light, left at second traffic light onto Division.
Phone: (401) 726–2080
Hours: 9:30 A.M.–4:00 P.M., Monday–Friday; 9:30 A.M.–12:30 P.M., Saturday. Closed week after Christmas and week of July 4th.
Credit Cards: No
Personal Checks: Yes, with proper identification
Handicapped Accessible: No
Bus Tours: Yes

Wakefield

Cherry Lane (Cannon)
14 Charles Street in the Cherry Branch Shopping Center

Directions: Route 1 to Wakefield. Outlet is 1 block south and west of the main intersection in Wakefield, the junction of Route 108 and Main Street.

Phone: (401) 789–7816
Hours: 9:00 A.M.–6:00 P.M., Monday–Thursday; 9:00 A.M.–8:00 P.M., Friday; 9:00 A.M.–5:00 P.M., Saturday; noon–4:00 P.M., Sunday
Credit Cards: No
Personal Checks: Yes, with proper identification
Handicapped Accessible: Yes
Bus Tours: Yes

West Warwick

Pepperidge Farms
Quaker Valley Mall
Quaker Lane (Route 2)

Directions: Call ahead.
Phone: (401) 828–3070
Hours: 10:00 A.M.–6:00 P.M., Monday–Wednesday; 10:00 A.M.–8:00 P.M., Thursday–Friday; 10:00 A.M.–5:00 P.M., Saturday
Credit Cards: No
Personal Checks: Yes, United States, with proper identification
Handicapped Accessible: Yes
Bus Tours: Yes

Woonsocket

Mark Stevens Warehouse
Woonsocket Plaza
Route 114 (Diamond Hill Road)

Directions: Route 114 to the Woonsocket Plaza.
Phone: (401) 766–4481
Hours: 9:00 A.M.–9:00 P.M., Monday–Saturday; 10:00 A.M.–6:00 P.M., Sunday
Credit Cards: American Express, Discover, MasterCard, Visa
Personal Checks: Yes, with proper identification

Handicapped Accessible: Yes
Restaurants: McDonald's
Bus Tours: Yes

Stitchers
1081 Social Street

Directions: Route 146, 122, or 114 to Route 126 (Social Street). Outlet on corner of Routes 114 and 126.
Phone: (401) 767–1500
Hours: 8:00 A.M.–3:30 P.M., Monday–Wednesday and Friday; 8:00 A.M.–5:00 P.M., Thursday; 8:00 A.M.–noon, Saturday
Credit Cards: No
Personal Checks: Yes, with proper identification
Handicapped Accessible: No
Bus Tours: No

Tinsel Town (Patioland)
93 Hazel Street

Directions: Route 126 (Social Street), right onto Pond Street, right onto East School Street, left onto Hazel Street.
Phone: (401) 766–5700
Hours: January to Thanksgiving: 9:00 A.M.–5:00 P.M., Monday–Saturday; noon–5:00 P.M., Sunday; Thanksgiving to December 31: 10:00 A.M.–9:00 P.M., Monday–Saturday; noon–6:00 P.M., Sunday
Credit Cards: MasterCard, Visa
Personal Checks: Yes, with proper identification
Handicapped Accessible: No
Bus Tours: Yes

Turfer Jacket
565 North Main Street

Directions: Route 146, 114, or 122 to Social Street in downtown Woonsocket. Right at North Main Street.

Phone: (401) 766–1088
Hours: 9:30 A.M.–4:00 P.M., Monday–Wednesday; 9:30 A.M.–8:00 P.M., Thursday; 9:30 A.M.–4:00 P.M., Friday; extended winter hours
Credit Cards: MasterCard, Visa
Personal Checks: Yes, with proper identification
Handicapped Accessible: No
Bus Tours: Yes

Remember that outlets accepting personal checks usually require at least two forms of proper identification, usually a driver's license and a major credit card.

Vermont

Numbers at the left of this legend correspond to the numbers on the accompanying map. The number to the right of each city's or town's name is the page number on which that municipality's outlets first appear in this book.

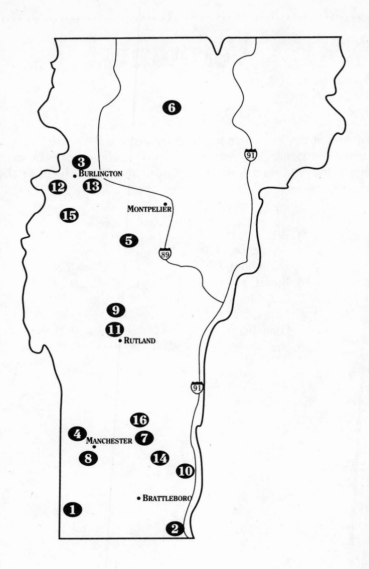

Bennington

Bennington Potters
324 County Street

Directions: Route 7 North from Routes 7 and 9 intersection, left onto County Street.
Phone: (802) 447–7531
Hours: 9:30 A.M.–5:30 P.M., Monday–Saturday; noon–5:30 P.M., Sunday; extended seasonal hours
Credit Cards: American Express, MasterCard, Visa
Personal Checks: Yes, with proper identification
Bus Tours: Yes

Catamount Glass
County Street

Directions: Across from Bennington Potters.
Phone: (802) 442–5438
Hours: 11:00 A.M.–4:30 P.M., Monday–Friday
Credit Cards: American Express, MasterCard, Visa
Personal Checks: Yes, with proper identification
Handicapped Accessible: Yes
Bus Tours: Yes

CB Sports
190 North Street

Directions: Next to A&P.
Phone: (802) 447–7651
Hours: 10:00 A.M.–5:00 P.M., Monday–Thursday and Saturday; 10:00 A.M.–6:00 P.M., Friday; noon–5:00 P.M., Sunday
Credit Cards: American Express, MasterCard, Visa
Personal Checks: Yes, with proper identification
Handicapped Accessible: Yes
Bus Tours: Yes

Dexter Shoe
121 Northside Drive

Directions: One-half mile north of Route 7 interchange.
Phone: (802) 447–1087
Hours: 9:30 A.M.–8:00 P.M., Monday–Saturday; 10:00 A.M.–5:00 P.M., Sunday
Credit Cards: MasterCard, Visa
Personal Checks: Yes, with proper identification
Handicapped Accessible: Yes
Bus Tours: Yes

Brattleboro

The Outlet Center
Canal Street (Route 5)

Directions: Exit 1 off I–91 onto Route 5 (Canal Street).
Phone: (802) 254–4594
Hours: 9:00 A.M.–9:00 P.M., Monday–Saturday; 10:00 A.M.–6:00 P.M., Sunday
Bus Tours: Yes
Outlets:
Amherst Sports
Bass
Carter's
Corning/Revere
Factory Handbag Store
The Last Straw
L'eggs/Hanes/Bali
Mary Meyer
Van Heusen
Westport, Ltd.

Burlington

Timberland
191 Bank Street

Directions: Call ahead.
Phone: (802) 862–2837
Hours: 10:00 A.M.–6:00 P.M., Monday–Thursday; 10:00 A.M.–9:00 P.M., Friday–Saturday; noon–5:00 P.M., Sunday; extended summer hours
Credit Cards: American Express, Discover, MasterCard, Visa
Personal Checks: Yes, with proper identification
Handicapped accessible: Yes
Bus Tours: No

Woodbury's of Shelburne
24 Church Street

Directions: Call ahead.
Phone: (802) 985–3742
Hours: 9:00 A.M.–6:00 P.M., Monday–Saturday; 10:00 A.M.–5:00 P.M., Sunday
Credit Cards: MasterCard, Visa
Personal Checks: Yes, with proper identification.
Handicapped Accessible: No
Bus Tours: Yes

Dorset

J. K. Adams
Route 30

Directions: Route 7 North to Manchester Center to Route 30, north to Dorset.
Phone: (802) 362–2303
Hours: 9:00 A.M.–5:30 P.M., Monday–Sunday
Credit Cards: American Express, Discover, MasterCard, Visa

Personal Checks: Yes, with proper identification
Handicapped Accessible: Yes
Bus Tours: Yes

Granville

Je-Mel Wood Products
Route 100

Directions: Route 100 to Granville and the store.
Phone: (802) 767–3266
Hours: 9:00 A.M.–5:00 P.M., Monday–Sunday
Features: Look for special wooden gifts here. The staff is very helpful and informative.
Credit Cards: Discover, MasterCard, Visa
Personal Checks: Yes, with proper identification
Handicapped Accessible: Yes
Bus Tours: Yes

Vermont Wood Specialties
Route 100

Directions: Route 100 to Granville and the store.
Phone: (802) 767–4253
Hours: 9:00 A.M.–5:00 P.M., Monday–Sunday
Credit Cards: Discover, MasterCard, Visa
Personal Checks: Yes, with proper identification
Handicapped Accessible: No
Bus Tours: Yes

Johnson

Johnson Woolen Mills
Main Street

Directions: I–89 to Waterbury exit. Northeast on Route 100 to Morrisville, left to Route 15 (Main Street).
Phone: (802) 635–2271
Hours: 8:00 A.M.–5:00 P.M., Monday–Friday; 9:00 A.M.–4:00 P.M., Saturday; 11:00 A.M.–4:00 P.M., Sunday, August–March only
Credit Cards: Discover, MasterCard, Visa
Personal Checks: Yes, with proper identification
Handicapped Accessible: Yes
Bus Tours: Yes

Londonderry

New England Shoe Barn
Routes 11 and 100

Directions: Store is at the intersection of Routes 11 and 100.
Phone: (802) 824–3737
Hours: 10:00 A.M.–5:30 P.M., Monday–Saturday; 10:00 A.M.–5:00 P.M., Sunday
Credit Cards: MasterCard, Visa
Personal Checks: Yes, with proper identification
Handicapped Accessible: No
Bus Tours: No

Manchester

Bass
Meadows Lane

Directions: From Manchester Center take Route 7A South.
Phone: (802) 362–4384
Hours: 9:00 A.M.–9:00 P.M., Monday–Saturday; 10:00 A.M.–6:00 P.M., Sunday
Credit Cards: American Express, Discover, MasterCard, Visa
Personal Checks: Yes, with proper identification
Handicapped Accessible: Yes

Crockett Collection
Manchester Industrial Park, Route 7A

Directions: Take Route 7A north of Manchester Center.
Phone: (802) 362–2913
Hours: 10:00 A.M.–5:00 P.M. Monday–Saturday
Features: Visitors can tour the shop where greeting cards are made.
Credit Cards: No
Personal Checks: Yes, with proper identificaiton
Handicapped Accessible: Yes
Bus Tours: Yes

Dexter Shoe
Route 11/30

Directions: One mile east of Route 7 junction.
Phone: (802) 362–4810
Hours: 9:30 A.M.–6:00 P.M., Monday–Saturday; 10:00 A.M.–5:00 P.M., Sunday; extended summer hours
Credit Cards: MasterCard, Visa
Personal Checks: Yes, with proper identification
Handicapped Accessible: Yes
Bus Tours: Yes

Knitty Gritty
Route 7A

Directions: Route 7A to Factory Point Square.
Phone: (802) 362–1157
Hours: 10:00 A.M.–5:30 P.M., Monday–Sunday
Credit Cards: MasterCard, Visa
Personal Checks: Yes, with proper identification
Handicapped Accessible: No
Bus Tours: Yes

* Manchester Center

Directions: The outlet stores and malls in Manchester are clustered around the intersection of Route 7A and Route 11/30 and continue along Route 11/30. Most are within walking distance of one another and are thus grouped together here.

For information on individual stores located in Manchester Center, call the Manchester and the Mountains Chamber of Commerce at (802) 362–2100. They have a complete listing of stores.
Hours: 10:00 A.M.–6:00 P.M., Monday–Sunday; some stores have extended hours
Outlet Malls:
Equinox Square
Manchester Commons
Manchester Marketplace
Manchester Square
Outlets:
Adrienne Vittadini
Anne Klein
Benetton
Boston Traders
Brooks Brothers
Calvin Klein
CB Sports
Christian Dior

Coach
Cole-Haan Shoes
Colours by Alexander Julian
Crabtree and Evelyn
Donna Karan
Ellen Tracy
Esprit
First Choice
Genuine Kids
Giorgio Armani
Go> Silk
HE-RO Group
Hickey-Freeman
Izod/Gant
J. Crew
Johnston & Murphy
Jones New York
Leather Loft
Liz Claiborne
London Fog
Maidenform
Manchester Wood
Mark Cross
Movado
9 West
Polly Flinders
Polo/Ralph Lauren
Seiko
Timberland
TSE Cashmere

Attractions: While you're in Manchester, visit the Orvis retail store, a must for sports enthusiasts, especially fishermen.

Mendon

Sweatertown U.S.A.
Route 4 East

Directions: Route 4 East, 7 miles from Routes 4 and 7 intersection.
Phone: (802) 773–7358
Hours: 9:30 A.M.–5:30 P.M., Monday–Sunday
Credit Cards: American Express, Discover, MasterCard, Visa
Personal Checks: Yes, with proper identification
Handicapped Accessible: Yes
Bus Tours: Yes

Putney

Green Mountain Spinnery
Depot Road

Directions: Exit 4 off I–91. Route 5 to Depot Road.
Phone: (802) 387–4528
Hours: 9:00 A.M.–5:30 P.M., Monday–Friday; 10:00 A.M.–5:30 P.M., Saturday
Credit Cards: MasterCard, Visa
Personal Checks: Yes, with proper identification
Handicapped Accessible: Yes
Bus Tours: Yes

Rutland

Dexter Shoe
Route 4

Directions: Four miles east of junction of Routes 4 and 7.
Phone: (802) 775–4370
Hours: 9:30 A.M.–6:00 P.M., Monday–Saturday; 10:00 A.M.–5:00 P.M., Sunday; extended summer hours

Credit Cards: MasterCard, Visa
Personal Checks: Yes, with proper identification
Handicapped Accessible: Yes
Bus Tours: Yes

Shelburne

Dexter Shoe
Shelburne Road

Directions: Route 7 becomes Shelburne Road in Shelburne.
Phone: (802) 985–8582
Hours: 9:00 A.M.–8:00 P.M., Monday–Saturday; 11:00 A.M.–6:00 P.M., Sunday; shorter summer hours
Credit Cards: MasterCard, Visa
Personal Checks: Yes, with proper identification
Handicapped Accessible: Yes
Bus Tours: Yes
Attractions: Plan to visit the Shelburne Museum. This array of buildings and objects will delight every member of the family. You'll love the beautiful interiors, paintings, and decorative arts; call (802) 985–3344 for information.

Vermont Teddy Bear Common
2031 Shelburne Road (Route 7)

Directions: Shelburne Road is Route 7.
Phone: (802) 985–8057
Hours: 9:00 A.M.–6:00 P.M., Monday–Thursday; 9:00 A.M.–9:00 P.M., Friday–Saturday; 10:00 A.M.–6:00 P.M., Sunday
Handicapped Accessible: Yes
Outlets:
Bass
Van Heusen

South Burlington

The Outlet Center
516 Shelburne Road, Route 7

Directions: Route 7 at junction with Route 189.
Phone: (802) 863–6037
Hours: 9:30 A.M.–9:30 P.M., Monday–Saturday; 11:00 A.M.–5:00 P.M., Sunday
Outlets:
Bass
Linens 'n Things
The Old Mill

Townshend

Townshend Furniture Company
Route 30

Directions: Route 30 North from Brattleboro to the store.
Phone: (802) 365–7720
Hours: 10:00 A.M.–4:30 P.M., Monday–Sunday
Credit Cards: MasterCard, Visa
Personal Checks: Yes, with proper identification
Handicapped Accessible: No
Bus Tours: Yes

Vergennes

Kennedy Brothers Woodenware
11 Main Street

Directions: Route 7 into Vergennes to Route 22A (Main Street).
Phone: (802) 877–2975
Hours: 9:00 A.M.–6:00 P.M., Monday–Sunday

Credit Cards: American Express, Discover, MasterCard, Visa
Personal Checks: Yes, with proper identification
Handicapped Accessible: Yes
Bus Tours: Yes

Weston

Weston Bowl Mill and Annex
Route 100

Directions: Route 100 to Weston and the store. ·
Phone: (802) 824–6219
Hours: 9:00 A.M.–5:00 P.M., Monday–Saturday; 9:00 A.M.–5:00 P.M., Sunday
Credit Cards: MasterCard, Visa
Personal Checks: Yes, with proper identification
Handicapped Accessible: No
Bus Tours: Yes

---

*Can't remember what product a particular outlet offers? Check our
"Profiles" section beginning on page one. Many listings also contain
information on brand names and range of discounts.*

Product Index

Accessories, Men's
(*See also* Clothing, Men's)
London Fog, 28
Mark Cross, 30
Stetson Hat, 38
Swank, 39
totes, 41

Accessories, Women's
(*See also* Clothing, Women's)
Accessory Factory, 1
Coach, 10
Dooney & Bourke, 15
London Fog, 28
Stetson Hat, 38
totes, 41
Trina, 41
Whiting and Davis, 45

Appliances, Small Electric
Black & Decker, 6
J. C. Penney, 22
Kitchen Collection/Proctor
Silex/Wearever, 25
Mark Cross, 30
Waring, 43

Athletic Clothing and Footwear
Bogner, 6
B.U.M., 7
Champion/Hanes, 9
Converse, 11
Fila, 18

nautica, 32
New Balance, 32
Pro Golf Discount, 35
Reebok/Rockport, 35
Saucony Soft-Bilt, 37

Audio/Stereo
Bose, 6
Magnavox, 29

Books
Book and Music Outlet, 6
Book Warehouse, 6

Candles, Soaps
Colonial Candle, 10
Crabtree and Evelyn, 12
Welcome Home, 44
Yankee Candle, 46

China, Crystal, Dinnerware, Cookware, Gifts
(*See also* Wood Products)
Alessi & Bourgeat, 1
Bennington Potters, 5
Catamount Glass, 8
Chicago Cutlery, 9
China Fair Warehouse, 9
Connecticut Gift, 11
Corning/Revere, 11
Crate and Barrel, 12
Dansk, 13
Dining In, 14

Mall Index

Outlet Index

Adams Mill
NH: Bedford, 138

Adolfo II
MA: Bourne, 101

Adrienne Vittadini
ME: Kittery, 88
VT: Manchester, 175

Aileen
CT: Branford, 49
    Mystic, 60
MA: East Falmouth, 105
    Fall River, 108
    Sagamore, 125
    West Yarmouth, 132
NH: North Hampton, 151

Alessi & Bourgeat
MA: New Bedford, 118

Alpine Sheets and Towels
ME: Freeport, 81

American Broadloom Braided Rug and Furniture Company
RI: Central Falls, 160

American Home Sewing
MA: Ware, 130

American Tourister
CT: Branford, 49
ME: Freeport, 81

Kittery, 88
MA: North Dartmouth, 120
    Sagamore, 125
NH: Conway, 147
    North Hampton, 151

Amherst Sports
VT: Brattleboro, 170

Anne Klein
ME: Freeport, 80
    Kittery, 88
MA: New Bedford, 118
NH: North Conway, 147
VT: Manchester Center, 175

Ann Taylor
MA: Worcester, 134

Arrow
ME: Freeport, 81
    Kittery, 86

Arrow Paper Party Store
CT: Groton, 55
    Madison, 57
    New London, 62
    Norwich, 66

The Artisan Outlet
NH: Portsmouth, 152

Bag and Baggage
CT: Norwalk, 64
ME: Freeport, 80

Bed & Bath
ME: Freeport, 81
NH: North Conway, 150
      North Hampton, 151

Bed, Bath, and Beyond
CT: Norwalk, 64
MA: Worcester, 134

Benetton
MA: Worcester, 134
ME: Freepprt, 81
VT: Manchester Center, 175

Bennington Potters
VT: Bennington, 169

Bidermann
MA: New Bedford, 118

Big Dog
NH: Tilton, 154

Black & Decker
CT: Orange, 68
ME: Kittery, 88
MA: North Dartmouth, 121

Bogner
ME: Freeport, 80, 81

Bon Worth
MA: North Dartmouth, 121

Book and Music Outlet
ME: Kittery, 86
NH: North Hampton, 151

Book Warehouse
ME: Kittery, 84
NH: Tilton, 154

Bose
ME: Kittery, 86

Boston Traders
ME: Freeport, 81
      Kittery, 89
MA: Lenox, 114
      Worcester, 134
NH: North Conway, 146
VT: Manchester Center,
      175

Brooks Brothers
ME: Freeport, 81
      Kittery, 88
NH: Tilton, 154
VT: Manchester Center, 175

Bugle Boy
ME: Freeport, 81
      Kittery, 87
MA: Fall River, 108
      Sagamore, 125

B.U.M.
MA: Worcester, 134
NH: Tilton, 155

Buttons and Things
ME: Freeport, 81

Calvin Klein
ME: Freeport, 81
      Kittery, 88

J. C. Penney
CT: Manchester, 58

J. Crew
ME: Freeport, 82
    Kittery, 84
NH: North Conway, 149
    Tilton, 155
VT: Manchester Center,
    176

Je-Mel Wood Products
VT: Granville, 172

Jennifer Convertibles
CT: Branford, 49

Jewelry Mine
ME: Kittery, 89

J. H. Collectibles
ME: Kittery, 89

J. K. Adams
VT: Dorset, 171

Joan & David
MA: Worcester, 134
NH: North Conway, 148

Jockey
MA: Worcester, 134
NH: Tilton, 155

John Henry and Friends
NH: North Conway, 149
    Tilton, 155

Johnson Woolen Mills
VT: Johnson, 173

Johnston & Murphy
ME: Freeport, 82
VT: Manchester Center, 176

Jonathan Logan
MA: North Dartmouth, 121
NH: Conway, 140

Jones New York
CT: Branford, 49
ME: Freeport, 82
    Kittery, 84
MA: New Bedford, 118
    Worcester, 134
VT: Manchester Center,
    176

Just Coats and Swimwear
CT: Branford, 49
    East Norwalk, 64
MA: Sturbridge, 128

Keene Mill End Store
NH: Keene, 143

**Kennedy Brothers
Woodenware**
VT: Vergennes, 179

**Kitchen Collection/Proctor-
Silex/Wearever**
ME: Kittery, 85
NH: North Conway, 147
    Tilton, 155

Deep Discounter Appendix

ABC Retail
ABC Retail specializes in apparel for juniors and misses and is located in:

Massachusetts:
Boston
Braintree
Burlington
Fall River
Foxboro
Framingham
Leominster
Pittsfield
Saugus
Seekonk
Weymouth
Worcester

Rhode Island:
Warwick

Anderson-Little
Anderson Little carries tailored business suits and separates for men and women and is located in:

Connecticut:
East Haven
East Norwalk
East Windsor
Hamden
Manchester
Newington
Norwalk
Orange
Waterbury

Massachusetts:
Auburn
Brockton
Burlington
Danvers
Dedham
Fall River
Franklin
Hingham
Leominster
Medford
Methuen
New Bedford
Newton
South Attleboro
Springfield
Swansea
West Springfield

New Hampshire:
Nashua

Rhode Island:
Lincoln
Warwick

Christmas Tree Shops

Christmas Tree Shops specialize in housewares, home decor, and seasonal items. Shops are located in:

Connecticut:
Manchester

Massachusetts:
Avon
Falmouth
Hyannis
Lynnefield
Orleans
Pembroke
Sagamore
Shrewsbury
West Dennis
West Yarmouth
Yarmouthport

New Hampshire:
Salem

Rhode Island:
Newport
Warwick

Filene's Basement

Filene's Basement carries clothing and accessories for the entire family and is located in:

Connecticut:
Manchester
Orange
West Hartford

Maine:
Portland

Massachusetts:
Boston
Braintree
Burlington
Dedham
Framingham
Holyoke
Hyannis
Kingston
Newton
North Attleboro
Peabody
Saugus
Taunton
Watertown
Wellesley
Worcester

New Hampshire:
Manchester
Nashua
Salem

Marshalls and T J maxx

Marshalls and T J maxx offer clothing, accessories, and footwear for men, women, and children. Also a selection of giftware, tableware, linens, and luggage.
Marshalls is located in:

Connecticut:
Avon
Bristol
Cheshire
Derby
Enfield
Hamden

Manchester
Meriden
Milford
New London
Southington
Waterbury
Watertown
West Hartford
Wethersfield

Maine:
South Portland

Massachusetts:
Andover
Bedford
Boston
Brockton
Burlington
Canton
Chelmsford
Danvers
Dorchester
Framingham
Franklin
Haverhill
Hingham
Hyannis
Leominster
Marlborough
Marshfield
Medford
Newburyport
Newton
North Attleboro
Plymouth
Raynham
Reading
Saugus

South Dennis
South Weymouth
Springfield
Stoneham
Swampscott
Swansea
Tewksbury
Watertown
Worcester

New Hampshire:
Bedford
Londonderry
Nashua
Portsmouth
Rochester
Salem

Rhode Island:
Cranston
East Providence
North Kingstown

T J maxx is located in:
Connecticut:
Bristol
Brookfield
Clinton
East Hartford
East Haven
Farmington
Groton
Hartford
Naugatuck
Newtown
North Haven
Norwalk
Norwich
Orange

Shelton
Southington
Torrington
Vernon
Waterbury
Wethersfield

Maine:
Auburn
Augusta
Bangor
South Portland

Massachusetts:
Ashland
Auburn
Bedford
Braintree
Cambridge
Chelmsford
Dedham
Falmouth
Franklin
Hudson
Hyannis
Leominster
Medford
Milford
North Andover
North Dartmouth
Norwood
Peabody
Pembroke
Pittsfield
Quincy
Saugus
Seekonk
South Attleboro
Springfield

Stoughton
Sudbury
Swampscott
Taunton
Tyngsboro
Waltham
Westboro
West Springfield
Wilmington
West Peabody
Worcester

New Hampshire:
Gilford
Londonderry
Manchester
Paistow
Portsmouth
Salem
Seabrook
Somersworth

Rhode Island:
Newport
North Kingston
Warwick

Vermont:
South Burlington